Preface

Apache Spark has already become the most popular cluster computing framework among companies and individuals. The framework embeds a unified analytics engine for large-scale data processing in order to target big data analytics and execute data science algorithms on large data sets. Apache Spark is highly flexible from an implementation perspective, you can write Spark programs in multiple languages including Java, Scala, Python, and SQL, which is why it is able to attract massive interest from a large developer community.

Partitioning is one of the basic building blocks on which the Spark framework has been built. You might not appreciate it much for smaller data sets. However, as you process larger data sets, partitioning at various stages of your program plays a very important role in ensuring the reliability, scalability, and efficiency of the programs. In fact, just setting the right partitioning across various stages, a lot of spark programs can be optimized right away.

We have encountered Apache Spark around 4 years back, and since then, we have been architecting Spark applications meant for executing complex data processing flow on massively sized multiple data sets. During all these years of architecting numerous Spark Jobs and working with a big team of Spark developers, we have found, in general, that the comprehensive understanding of various aspects of Spark partitioning lacks among Spark users, causing them to lose on the massive optimization opportunities for building a reliable, efficient and scalable Spark Jobs meant for processing larger data sets.

Therefore, based on our experience, knowledge, and research, we decided to write this book focusing just on this one important aspect of Apache Spark, i.e., partitioning. The book's title, "Guide to Spark Partitioning" is also aligned with this single objective of the book. Chapter 1 of the book introduces you to the concept of partitioning and its importance. Chapter 2 goes into depth to explain partitioning rules while reading ingested data files. Chapter 3 goes into depth to explain partitioning rules for Spark transformations that affect partitioning structure. Chapter 4 focusses on explicit partitioning APIs, various re-partition APIs and the coalesce API. Chapter 5, the last chapter, provides details on how the partitions are written on to a permanent storage medium.

Further, the book focusses primarily on the RDD and Dataset representation of the data that is available in the recent versions of the Spark. To aid in understanding the concepts presented in the chapter, we have also provided many examples in every chapter of the book. Further, any effect of adaptive query execution (introduced in the latest Spark 3.0 announced in May 2020) feature on partitioning is currently not considered in the book. We are planning to add an additional chapter on the same in the next revision of the book once the adoption to Spark 3.0 becomes a bit popular.

Acknowledgements

First and foremost, we would like to thank our department head, Aayush Bhatnagar. Without the support and motivation from him, the book would have not been possible. He has guided & mentored us all the way in our Spark Journey. We are indebted to him for providing us the opportunity to work on the fascinating and challenging world of Big Data analytics. Lastly, we would like to thank friends, family and loved ones. Without their support and patience, we would not have been able to write the book.

Ajay Kumar Gupta
(Engineering Manager & Big Data Architect, Jio Platforms Limited)

Naushad Ahamad
(Senior Big Data Developer, Jio Platforms Limited)

Table of Contents

PARTITIONING IN SPARK..1

Partition 1

Visualizing Partitions 2

Partitioning...4

Hash Partitioning 4

Range Partitioning 5

Partitioning in RDDs..6

Partitioning in Datasets...10

Why Partitioning is important? 12

INPUT PARTITIONS FROM DATA FILES 17

Bucket Specification..18

Splittable File Formats 19

Configurable Parameters Affecting Input Partitions 20

Input Partitions of a Dataset from a set of Data Files without Bucketing
specification 21

Input Partitions of an RDD from a set of Data Files............29

Input Partitions of a Dataset from a set of Data Files with Bucketing
specification 37

PARTITIONING DURING SPARK TRANSFORMATIONS 39

Narrow Transformations..40

Wide Transformations 41

Output Partitioning for Spark Transformations 42

One-to-One Output Partitioning 42

Output Partitioning in Union...42

Output Partitioning in Aggregation 46

Output Partitioning in Joins 53

REPARTITION AND COALESCE 70

Repartition APIs...73

Repartition APIs Operation 77

Coalesce APIs..78

Coalesce API Operation...79

Repartition or Coalesce..79

PARTITIONING TO OUTPUT FILES...83

Basic Approach 84

PartitionBy Approach...86

bucketBy Approach..89

partitionBy, bucketBy Approach 92

Chapter 1

Partitioning in Spark

Partitioning, in Spark, refers to distribution of the data into logical compute chunks. This distribution of data is either completely random or based on a certain scheme, the scheme being called as partitioning scheme.

Partition

A Partition represents a single logical chunk of data of a larger data set which is logically distributed into one or more of such chunks. Computation for a single partition is executed by a single task scheduled to run on a single physical server. Therefore, the partition is also being referred to as the unit of parallelism in the Spark framework. Computations on multiple partitions of a data set can be executed in parallel by multiple CPU cores distributed across multiple physical machines.

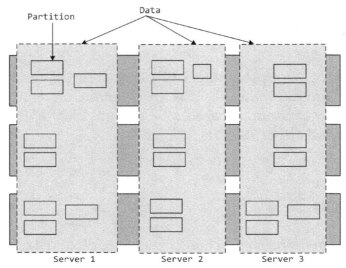

Figure 1.1: Partition as a logical chunk of data

Visualizing Partitions

Spark has provided friendly APIs to inspect the data in individual partitions and query the number of partitions contained in a data set. In Spark, each data set either is represented by a lowest level abstraction, called as RDD, or a higher-level abstraction called as Dataset. RDD represents data as a collection of raw data records whereas Dataset supports the structured view of underlying data.

To know the number of partitions directly in a raw RDD, you can use the following API on an RDD 'A':

```
Num_of_Partitions = A.getNumPartitions()
```

To get the data of all the partitions contained in a raw RDD, you can use the 'glom' on an RDD 'A' which would convert each partition into an array of data records contained in the corresponding partitions. The arrays can be collected on the driver afterwards using:

```
A.glom().collect()
```

Example 1.1

```
num_partitions = 15

A = spark.sparkContext.parallelize(range(10),
num_partitions)

print('Number of partitions:
{}'.format(A.getNumPartitions()))

print('Partitions structure:
{}'.format(A.glom().collect()))
```

Output for Example 1.1:

```
Number of partitions: 15
Partitions structure: [[], [1], [0], [], [3], [2], [],
[4], [5], [], [6], [7], [], [8], [9]]
```

To get similar information on partitions in case of a Dataset, you can use 'getNumPartitions' and 'glom' APIs on the underlying RDD of a Dataset which is accessible via the following API:

```
A.rdd()
```

Partitioning

As stated earlier, Partitioning in Spark refers to the scheme of distribution of data contained in a data set across a set of partitions designated for the data set. There are two important aspects of this scheme:

- Number of partitions in which the data is distributed
- How the data is distributed across the chosen number of partitions.

Partitioning can be completely random or round-robin type where a data record is randomly assigned to designated partitions just to attain uniform distribution. Also, Partitioning can also be very-very specific where each data record of the data set always maps to a fixed partition out of 'n' partitions decided for the data set. Here are the two examples of the specific partitioning being widely used in Spark.

Hash Partitioning

In the Hash Partitioning scheme, a data record is placed in a partition based on the hash value evaluated for the data record. In the case of raw Pair RDDs, the hash value is evaluated as the hash code of the Key specified for the data record. While, in the case of Datasets, the hash value is evaluated as the hash of the value of an expression made of one or more fields of the data record.

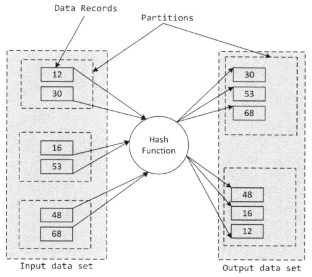

Fig.1.2: Hash Partitioning executed for a Spark data set

Range Partitioning

In the Range partitioning scheme, first of all, a range is determined for each of the partitions. The range is based on either the sortable values of keys in case of a Pair RDD, or on sortable values of an expression of one or more data fields in the case of a Dataset.

To determine the range for each of the partitions, the data to be range partitioned is sampled to construct a view of the global range of sortable values arranged either in an ascending or descending order. After the view is constructed, the global range is distributed across available distributions uniformly.

Once the range is determined for each of the partitions, for each of the data records, range determining sortable value is computed based on which it is then assigned to the appropriate partition whose range included the computed value.

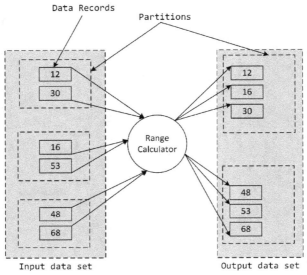

Fig. 1.3: Range Partitioning executed for a Spark data set

Partitioning in RDDs

Partitioning in an RDD which is representing data from an input data source is decided on prebuilt rules. These rules decide on the number of partitions of the input RDD and maps the data in each partition of the input RDD to a set of data records residing in the data source. This input source could either be a runtime collection of data records, a set of data files residing on a file system (such as HDFS), or a Table stored in a Database. Various aspects and rules of partitioning for RDDs built from input data sources are explained in detail in Chapter 2.

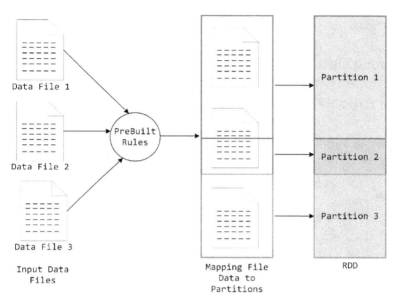

Fig. 1.4: Partitioning of an RDD representing data in Files using prebuilt rules

However, partitioning on existing RDDs is accomplished mostly with the assistance of a Partitioner utility. This utility can be built easily by implementing the abstract methods of the Partitioner class. But, Partitioners are only available for pair RDDs where each data record has an associated Key object.

Spark has already provided two readymade Partitioners for use by Spark developers, one is called HashPartitioner to achieve Hash Partitioning on the desired data set, and another is called RangePartitioner to achieve Range Partitioning on the desired data set.

Also, if you need to implement a different partitioning scheme for your data set, then you can optionally implement a custom Partitioner by extending and implementing the abstract functions of the Partitioner class. This is explained in detail in Chapter 4

Partitioning Info can also be supplied explicitly to RDD transformations requiring partitioning. Some of these explicit APIs accept only the one aspect of the partitioning info that is the number of partitions, while other APIs accept the whole Partitioner object. APIs accepting only the number of partitions usually choose a Hash Partitioner object to distribute the data in accordance with the number of partitions.

Once an implicit or explicit Partitioner is used to re-distribute the data, the used Partitioner gets associated with the output RDD produced by the transformation. The Partitioner associated with an RDD can be inspected using the following API applicable on an RDD 'A':

```
A.partitioner()
```

If there is no partitioner associated with an RDD, the partitioner API would print 'None', else it would print the relevant details of the Partitioner object. Spark uses the partitioner information of an RDD extensively in optimizing the operations of certain transformations. Like in the case of inner Join on two Pair RDDs, if both of the RDDs already have the same associated partitioner, the join operation essentially gets reduced to a narrow transformation thereby saving on the cost of shuffling of the two input RDDs.

However, there are certain RDD transformations which do not carry forward the Partitioner of the input RDD to the output RDD. One example of such a transformation is 'mapToPair' on a Pair RDD, the reason being the potential possibility of change in Key object itself for some data records during the course of transformation.

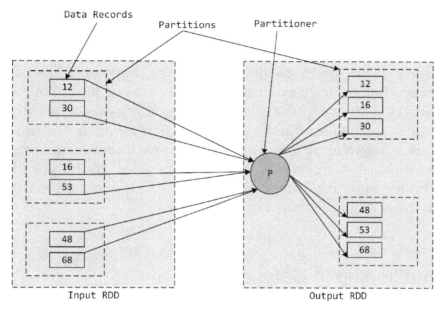

Fig. 1.5: Illustration of partitioning being executed on an existing RDD

If this such a change happens even for one record, and the Partitioner is carried forward to the output RDD, then the Partitioner as the part of output RDD would portray wrong information about the data distribution (in accordance with Key objects).

Therefore, to avoid such situations and maintain the predictability of the transformation, Input Partitioner is not carried forward to the output RDD of the transformation.

Apart from the data transformations that involve re-distribution of input data, Spark has provided transformation APIs to explicitly repartition the RDD data at will. These APIs too ask either for the number of partitions and assumes a

Hash Partitioner internally or they would ask for the Partitioner itself from the user. Details about these repartition APIs are provided in Chapter 4.

There is also a special API, called 'coalesce', provided to users to re-distribute the data into a specified number of output partitions, but this particular API takes a very special approach to attain re-distribution. The approach basically groups one or more existing partitions into one logical output partition. Meaning, the approach does not assign individual data records to an output partition using a Partitioner. Also, since it is re-mapping of multiple input partitions to an output partition, this approach can only be used to reduce the number of partitions in an existing RDD. More about the Coalesce API is provided in Chapter 4.

Partitioning in Datasets

A Dataset in Spark represents structured data as opposed to RDD which represents raw unstructured records. As in the case of RDD, partitioning in a Dataset representing data from an input data source is decided on prebuilt rules. These rules decide on the number of partitions of the Dataset and maps the data in each partition of the Dataset to a set of data records residing in the data source. Various aspects and rules of partitioning from input data sources in the case of Datasets are also explained in detail in Chapter 2.

Further, similar to RDD, data in an existing Dataset gets re-distributed on invoking Dataset specific APIs. The Dataset APIs, however, are not as flexible as in the case of RDDs. Like, for example, APIs such as 'agg' and 'join', meant for aggregation and joins transformations respectively, re-distributes the records in input Dataset(s) when the distribution of the input Datasets(s) don't match the distribution semantics of the underlying transformation/operation represented by the APIs. However, the APIs don't ask for any of the partitioning aspect from the user. In case, a re-distribution is necessitated, the number of partitions and the distribution scheme are chosen by a set of rules designated for different operations. These set of rules are explained in detail in Chapter 3.

The explicit re-partitioning APIs available in the case of Datasets asks the user for the number of partitions (for the re-distribution of data) and the partitioning expression which is made up of one or more fields of structured data represented by the input Dataset. The re-partitioning APIs are available in two flavors, one performs partitioning using the hash partitioning approach while the other one uses the range partitioning approach. However, there are no Dataset APIs where a user can specify a custom partitioning approach as in case of RDDs. More on the re-partition APIs of Datasets is covered in Chapter 4.

When the records in a Dataset get re-partitioned, the corresponding partitioning approach is recorded in the Dataset. The recording of the partitioning approach for a Dataset helps in eliminating the re-partitioning of the Dataset on the similar recorded approach warranted by a subsequent transformation(s) operating the Dataset.

Further, on the lines coalesce APIs available for RDDs, Dataset also supports a similar coalesce API which only re-maps the partitions as a whole in the input Dataset to decrease the number of output partitions without re-distributing the individual data records in the input partitions to the output partitions.

Why Partitioning is important?

Partitioning is very important because the whole framework of Spark execution is built around it. From the top, the Spark execution is divided into one or more computational stages, where each stage either computes partitions of an RDD or Dataset (from one or more partitions of previously computed RDD or Dataset) or executes an action on each of the partition. A stage accomplishes the same by scheduling a dedicated task for each of the partitions in an input data set.

Partitioning Affects Parallelism

A partition is computed by a single task configured to run with designated computing resources. Considering a set of cluster computing resources being allocated to Spark application, the Spark execution engine can schedule multiple

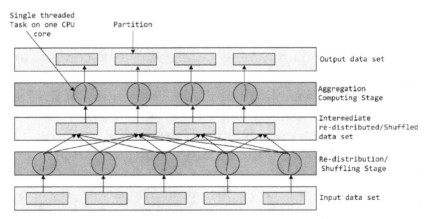

Fig. 1.6: Illustration of stage computation model in Spark for an Aggregate transformation

partition computing tasks (belonging to multiple stages that are ready for execution) in parallel. Therefore, it can be deduced that the first aspect of partitioning, i.e., the number of partitions directly affects the parallelism of a Spark application.

Partitioning Affects Resiliency

Failure in Spark is also understood at the partition level. While computing a partition of an intermediate data set, failure in computing of even a single data record fails the computation of the entire partition as a whole. To address failures in Spark, resiliency in Spark is also being built around partitions across multiple stages. When one or more partitions fail during a stage, only those particular partitions are being re-attempted for computation by scheduling corresponding tasks on the cluster. Also, during the re-attempt, if the dependent partitions in the previously computed datasets are not available then those dependent partitions are computed first in accordance with dependency lineage.

Partitioning Affects Data Shuffling

Re-distribution of data from previously computed partitions (of the previously computed dataset) to a newer set of partitions (belonging to a newly computed data set) involves disk read and write operations along with potential network transfers. This whole process of executing a re-distribution operation is termed as shuffling and a data block to be shuffled from one input partition to an output partition is termed as shuffle block.

Partitioning of an input data set or the output data set directly affects the partitioning procedure. If the number of input partitions is relatively lesser than the output ones, then the executors hosting the shuffle blocks can be potentially overwhelmed with shuffle fetch requests causing delay or unreliability to the underlying shuffle operation. On the other hand, if the number of output partitions is relatively lesser than the input partitions, then the tasks processing the completed shuffle fetch requests would get overwhelmed, again, causing delay or unreliability to the underlying shuffle operation.

Partitioning Affects Operations Efficiency

Some of the Spark operations require the data in the input data set to be re-distributed according to a certain scheme. If that is not the case, then the data in the input data set is first re-distributed by executing a shuffle operation before the actual operation goes into execution. However, if the data in the input data set is already distributed as mandated by the operation, then the extra shuffle operation gets eliminated and the operation becomes much more efficient.

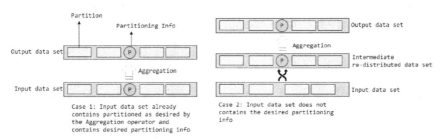

Figure 1.7: Effect of Presence of Partitioning Info on Input data sets

Partitioning Affects the RAM processing

Spark has provided some special APIs, such as 'mapPartitions' and 'foreachPartitions', which allows users to efficiently process a partition as a whole and not by the usual record wise APIs. Since, these special APIs computes on a partition level, the amount of RAM they demand is comparatively higher than in the usual case. Therefore, if the partitioning of input data set packs higher number of data records in a partition, use of the special APIs can get risky if the amount of RAM allocated is not in the same proportion.

Partitioning Affects Data Skew

Data Skew is used to describe the scenario of unbalanced data distributions across partitions. Meaning, few partitions carry way more data records as compared to others. Data Skew can result from the

Partitioning of an input data set when the underlying partitioning expression when evaluated for all the data records results in a skewed distribution of expression values. Data Skew in a data set causes subsequent operations on the same unreliable and inefficient. Therefore, partitioning of a data set should avoid data skew scenarios if the same is possible.

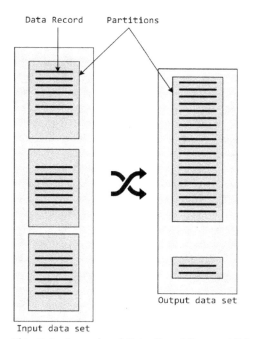

Fig. 1.8: Scenario of Data Skew After partitioning
a data set

Partitioning Affects Storage in Files

If the data records contained in a data set have to be written in a file, then Spark usually produces a part file for each partition contained in the data set. The same can cause trouble if the data set has large number of smaller-sized partitions in the data set, because then, it would produce large number of small-sized files equivalent to the large number of partitions. This could be a problem because each file occupies a space in the metadata of the associated file system.

Chapter 2
Input Partitions from Data Files

Most Spark applications source their input data (for their execution pipeline) from data files in various formats. To facilitate the reading of data from files, Spark has provided dedicated APIs in the context of both, raw RDDs and Datasets. These APIs abstract the reading process from data files to an input RDD or a Dataset with a definite number of partitions. You can then perform various transformations/actions on these inputs RDDs/Datasets.

Each of the partitions in an input raw RDD or a Dataset is mapped to one or more data files, the mapping being done either on a part of a file or on the entire file. During the execution of a Spark Job with an input RDD/Dataset in its pipeline, each of the partition of the input RDD/Dataset is computed by reading the data as per the mapping of partition to the data file(s). The computed partition data is then fed to dependent RDDs/Dataset further into the execution pipeline.

The number of partitions decided for the input RDD/Dataset could affect the efficiency of the entire execution pipeline of the Job. Therefore, it is important to know, how the number of partitions is decided, based on certain parameters, in case of an input RDD or a Dataset.

The number of partitions in an input RDD/Dataset (mapped to the data file(s)) is decided based on the bucket specification, the splittable property of a file, set of configurable parameters, and the sum of the size of the data files. Let us understand these factors in detail:

Bucket Specification

Bucket specification explicitly specifies the partitioning structure of a table backed by a corresponding set of files stored at the table path. Bucket specification is usually stored as the part of metadata of a table. A bucket specification is made of up three parameters:

- Number of Buckets
- Bucketing Columns names
- Sort Columns names

Number of Buckets and Bucketing column names are mandatory for a bucketing specification. The number of buckets specifies the output buckets for partitioning the data, while one or more bucketing columns names are mapped to the respective columns of the data.

A Bucket specification is created when you create a table via

```
'SPARK SQL' and specify 'CLUSTERED BY
(#Bucketing_Columns) INTO (#No_of_Buckets) BUCKETS'
```

expression mentioning one or more bucketing columns and the number of buckets. Once, a table is created in this way, writing data into the table would appropriately partition the data into the specified number of buckets and accordingly write the data files on the disk.

A Bucket specification is also created when you write the data into the table via DataFrameWriter and use the bucketBy API mentioning the number of buckets and the bucketing columns in the API.

Splittable File Formats

A File is said to be splittable when different parts of the same file can be processed in parallel. A splittable File format allows you to break a corresponding big File (based on the File format) in multiple parts and process these parts in parallel to achieve computational efficiency. Here is a table specifying the splittable format of popular File formats which are commonly used in Spark applications.

File Format	Compression/ Compression Type	Is Splittable ?
Parquet	No	Yes
Parquet	Yes / Any	Yes
ORC	No	Yes
ORC	Yes / Any	Yes
CSV (Each record spanning single line)	No	Yes
CSV (Each record spanning single line)	Yes / Non-Splittable	No
CSV (Each record spanning single line)	Yes / Splittable (such as bzip2)	Yes
CSV (Each record spanning multi lines)	No	No
CSV (Each record spanning multi lines)	Yes / Any	No
Json (Each record spanning single line)	No	Yes
Json (Each record spanning single line)	Yes / Non-Splittable	No
Json (Each record spanning single line)	Yes / Splittable (such as bzip2)	Yes
Json (Each record	No	No

spanning multi lines)		
Json (Each record spanning multi lines)	Yes / Any	No
Binary	No	No
Binary	Yes / Any	No
Generic Text File (Each record spanning single line)	No	Yes
Generic Text File (Each record spanning single line)	Yes / Non-Splittable	No
Generic Text File (Each record spanning single line)	Yes / Splittable (such as bzip2)	Yes
Generic Text File (Record spans whole File)	No	No
Generic Text File (Record spans whole File)	Yes / Any	No

File Splitability plays an important role in deciding on the number of input partitions while reading an RDD or Dataset from a set of data files.

Configurable Parameters Affecting Input Partitions

Following are the configurable parameters which affects the input partitions of a Dataset representing the Data in a set of data files:

- `'spark.default.parallelism'`: Spark specific configuration having default value equal to total number of CPU cores allocated to the Spark application.

- `'spark.sql.files.maxPartitionBytes'`: Spark specific configuration suggesting maximum bytes to be packed in a partition. It has a default value of 128 MB.

- `'spark.sql.files.openCostInBytes'` - Spark specific configuration suggesting the cost of opening a data file in MB. It has a default value of 4 MB.

- `'minSize (mapred.min.split.size)'` - This is one of the Hadoop configurations having default value of 1 MB

- `'blockSize (dfs.blocksize)'` – Again Hadoop specific configuration specifying the Hadoop block size. It has a default value of 128 MB.

Input Partitions of a Dataset from a set of Data Files without Bucketing specification

Multiple APIs are provided by Spark for reading data files into a Dataset, and each of these APIs is called on an instance of a SparkSession ('sparkSession') which forms a uniform entry point of a Spark application since version 2.0. Some of these APIs are shown below:

File Format specific APIs:
- `sparkSession.read.csv (String path or List of paths)`

- `sparkSession.read.json` (String path or List of paths)
- `sparkSession.read.text` (String path or List of paths)
- `sparkSession.read.parquet` (String path or List of paths)
- `sparkSession.read.orc` (String path or List of paths)

Generic API:

- `sparkSession.read.format(String fileformat).load(String path or List of paths)`

'path' in all the above APIs represents either the actual file path or directory path to a set of files. Also, it could contain wildcard, such as '*'. There are more variants of the above APIs which also includes the facility of specifying various options while reading the data file. Full list can be referred here:

`"https://spark.apache.org/docs/2.3.0/api/java/org/apache/spark/sql/DataFrameReader.html"`

Procedure for selecting the Input Partitions

Using the config parameters described earlier, a maximum split guideline called as **'maxSplitBytes'** is calculated as follows:

- `maxSplitBytes = Minimum ( maxPartitionBytes, bytesPerCore )`

- `bytesPerCore = (Sum of sizes of all data files + No. of files * openCostInBytes) / default.parallelism`

Then the file chunks are calculated for each of the data file by splitting each of the data files (to be read) using 'maxSplitBytes'. Therefore, if a file is splittable and the file size is more than 'maxSplitBytes', then the file is split in multiple chunks of 'maxSplitBytes', the last chunk being less than or equal to 'maxSplitBytes'. If the file is not splittable, or the file size is less than 'maxSplitBytes', then there is only one file chunk of size equivalent to the file size itself.

After the file chunks are identified for all the data files, one or more file chunks are packed in a partition. The packing process starts with initializing an empty partition first, followed by the iteration over the file chunks, for each iterated file chunk:

- If there is no current partition being packed, initialize a new partition to be packed and assign the iterated file chunk to it. The partition size becomes the sum of chunk size and the additional overhead of 'openCostInBytes'.

- If the addition of chunk size does not exceed the size of current partition (being packed) by more than 'maxSplitBytes', then the file chunk becomes the part of the current partition. The partition size is incremented by the sum of the chunk size and the additional overhead of 'openCostInBytes'.

- If the addition of chunk size exceeds the size of current partition, being packed, by more than 'maxSplitBytes', then the current partition is declared as complete and a new partition is initiated which becomes the current partition. The iterated file chunk becomes the part of the newer current partition, and the newer partition size becomes equal to the sum of chunk size and the additional overhead of 'openCostInBytes'.

After the packing process is over, the number of partitions of the Dataset, for reading the corresponding data files, is obtained. Although the process of arriving at the number of partitions seems to be a bit complicated, the basic idea,

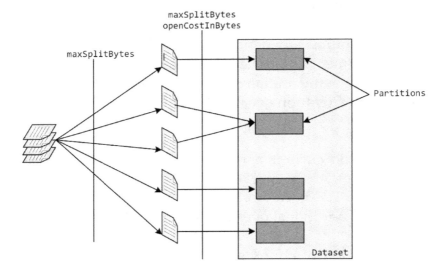

Fig. 2.1: Illustration of Procedure to split a set of input data files into the partition of a Dataset

according to Figure 2.1, is to first split the individual files at the boundary of 'maxSplitBytes' if the file is splittable. After which, the splitted chunks of files, or the unsplittable files are packed into a partition such that during packing of chunks into a partition, if the partition size exceeds 'maxSplitBytes', the partition is considered complete for packing, and a new partition is taken for packing. Thus, a certain number of partitions are finally derived out of the packing process.

Here are a few examples to make you understand this procedure correctly:

Example 2.1:

- No. of File to be read: 54
- File Format: parquet
- File Size: Each file of size 65 MB
- No. of cores: 10
- 'spark.default.parallelism' (default: Total No. of CPU cores: 10)
- 'spark.sql.files.maxPartitionBytes' (default: 128 MB)
- 'spark.sql.files.openCostInBytes' (default: 4 MB)

Explanation: The number of input partitions for the Example 2.1 are 54. 'maxSplitBytes' for this example comes out as 128 MB. Each file here has only one chunk in this case, and it is obvious here that two file chunks cannot be packed in one partition as the size would exceed 'maxSplitBytes' after adding the second file chunk. Therefore, the number of output partitions are 54.

Example 2.2:

- No. of File to be read: 54
- File Format: parquet
- File Size: Each file of size 63 MB
- No. of cores: 10
- 'spark.default.parallelism' (default: Total No. of CPU cores: 10)
- 'spark.sql.files.maxPartitionBytes' (default: 128 MB)
- 'spark.sql.files.openCostInBytes' (default: 4 MB)

Explanation: The number of input partitions for the Example 2.2 are also 54. 'maxSplitBytes' for this example comes out as 128 MB. Each of the file here also has only 1 file chunk. Here, it looks that two files can be packed here according to 'maxSplitBytes', but since, there is an overhead of 'openCostInBytes' (4 MB) after packing the first file, therefore, according to partition packing procedure, after adding the second file, the limit of 128 MB gets crossed, and hence, two files cannot be packed in one partition, and therefore the number of output partitions are equal to 54.

Example 2.3:

- No. of File to be read: 54
- File Format: parquet
- File Size: Each file of size 40 MB
- No. of cores: 10
- 'spark.default.parallelism' (default: Total No. of CPU cores: 10)
- 'spark.sql.files.maxPartitionBytes' (default: 128 MB)
- 'spark.sql.files.openCostInBytes' (default: 4 MB)

Explanation: The number of input partitions for Example 2.3 are 18. 'maxSplitBytes' for this example comes out as 128 MB. Each of the file here also has only 1 file chunk. According to the partition packing process, even after adding two files of 40 MB and overhead of 4 MB each for the two files, the total size comes out to be 88 MB only, therefore, the third file of 40 MB can also be packed since the size come out to be just 128 MB. Hence, the number of partitions comes out to be 18.

Note: An important point to be noted from Example 3.3 is that while evaluating the packing eligibility for the file chunk, overhead of 'openCostInBytes' is not considered, the overhead is considered only while incrementing the partition size after the file chunk is considered for packing in the partition.

Example 2.4:

- No. of File to be read: 54
- File Format: parquet
- File Size: Each file of size 40 MB
- No. of cores: 10
- 'spark.default.parallelism' (default: Total No. of CPU cores: 10)
- 'spark.sql.files.maxPartitionBytes' (default: 88 MB)
- 'spark.sql.files.openCostInBytes' (default: 4 MB)

Explanation: The number of input partitions for Example 2.4 are 27. This example reflects the effect of change in the config property, 'spark.sql.files.maxPartitionBytes' which is set to 88 MB explicitly. 'maxSplitBytes' for this example also comes out as 88 MB. Therefore, here, each of the file has only 1 file chunk. According to the partition packing process, two files can be packed in a single partition. Hence, , the number of partitions comes out to be 27.

Example 2.5:

- No. of File to be read: 54
- File Format: parquet
- File Size: Each file of size 40 MB
- No. of cores: 10
- 'spark.default.parallelism' (400)
- 'spark.sql.files.maxPartitionBytes' (default: 128 MB)
- 'spark.sql.files.openCostInBytes' (default: 4 MB)

Explanation: The number of input partitions for Example 2.5 are 378. This case reflects the effect of change in the config property, 'spark.default.parallelism' which is set to 400 explicitly. 'maxSplitBytes' for this example also comes out as 5.94 MB. Therefore, each of the file here has only 7 file chunks. According to the partition packing process, only one file chunk can be packed in a single partition. Hence, the number of partitions comes out to be 378.

Example 2.6:

- No. of File to be read: 10
- File Format: CSV (compressed with unsplittable compression codec, gzip)
- File Size: Each file of size 355 MB
- No. of cores: 10
- 'spark.default.parallelism' (default, equal to number of cores)
- 'spark.sql.files.maxPartitionBytes' (default: 128 MB)
- 'spark.sql.files.openCostInBytes' (default: 4 MB)

Explanation: The number of input partitions for Example 2.6 are 10. This case reflects the effect of unsplittable compression codec. Each of the file here has only 1 file chunk since the file is unsplittable. Also, according to the partition packing process, only one file chunk can be packed in a single partition. Hence, the number of partitions comes out to be 10.

Example 2.7:

- No. of File to be read: 10
- File Format: CSV (compressed with splittable compression codec, bzip2)
- File Size: Each file of size 311 MB
- No. of cores: 10
- 'spark.default.parallelism' (default, equal to number of cores)
- 'spark.sql.files.maxPartitionBytes' (default: 128 MB)
- 'spark.sql.files.openCostInBytes' (default: 4 MB)

Explanation: The number of input partitions for Example 2.7 are 25. This case reflects the effect of splittable compression codec. 'maxSplitBytes' for this example also comes out as 128 MB. Therefore, each of the file here has only 3 file chunks according to 'maxSplitBytes', since the file is splittable. Out of the three file chunks, 2 are of size 128 MB each whereas the 3rd one is of size 55 MB. Now, according to the partition packing process, 20 file chunks of 128 MB each of all 10 files can be packed in 20 partitions, while the remaining 10 files chunks of 55 MB each of all 10 files can be packed in 5 partitions. Hence, the number of partitions comes out to be 25.

Input Partitions of an RDD from a set of Data Files

Here are the examples of the APIs that are provided by Spark for reading data files into an RDD, each of these APIs is called on the SparkContex ('sparkContext') of a SparkSession instance:

- sparkContext.newAPIHadoopFile (String path, Class<F> fClass, Class<K> kClass, Class<V> vClass, org.apache.hadoop.conf.Configuration conf)
- sparkContext.textFile (String path, int minPartitions)
- sparkContext.sequenceFile (String path, Class<K> keyClass, Class<V> valueClass)
- sparkContext.sequenceFile (String path, Class<K> keyClass, Class<V> valueClass, int minPartitions)
- sparkContext.objectFile (String path, int minPartitions, scala.reflect.ClassTag<T> evidence$4)

In some of these APIs, a parameter 'minPartitions' is asked while in others it is not. If it is not asked, the default value for the same is taken as 2 or 1, 1 in the case when 'spark.default.parallelism' is 1. This 'minPartitions' is one of the factors in deciding the number of partitions in the RDD returned by these APIs.

To decide on the number of input partitions for an RDD, a split guideline, called split size ('splitSize'), is calculated using 'minPartitions' and the following configurable parameters:

- `minSize (mapred.min.split.size)`
- `blockSize (dfs.blocksize).`

The calculation is done as follows :

- `splitSize = Math.max ( minSize, Math.min(goalSize, blockSize))`

  `where:`

- `goalSize = Sum of all files lengths to be read / minPartitions`

Now using 'splitSize', each of the data files (to be read) is split if the same is splittable. Therefore, if a file is splittable with a size more than 'splitSize'. then the file is split in multiple chunks of 'splitSize', the last chunk being less than or equal to 'splitSize'. If the file is not splittable, or have size less then 'splitSize', then there is only one file chunk of size equal to the file length.

After all the file chunks are identified, each of the file chunks (having size greater than zero) is mapped to a single partition. Therefore, the number of partitions in the RDD, returned by

RDD APIs on data files, is equal to the number of non-zero file chunks derived from slicing the data files using 'splitSize'.

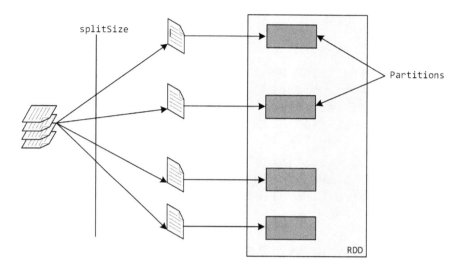

Fig. 2.2: Illustration of Procedure to split a set of input data files into the partition of a RDD

Here are the few examples to make you understand this procedure correctly:

Example 2.8:

- No. of File to be read: 31
- File Format: parquet
- File Size: Each file of size 330 MB
- No. of cores: 10
- 'minPartitions': Not specified
- 'mapred.min.split.size': (default: 1 MB)
- 'dfs.blocksize': (default: 128 MB)
- 'spark.default.parallelism': (default: Total No. of CPU cores: 10)

Explanation: The number partitions for Example 2.8 comes out as 93. The splitSize for this case comes out be 128 MB only, so basically, each file has 3 file chunks since parquet is splittable. Now, since each file chunk maps to single partition, the total partitions come out to be 93.

Example 2.9:

- No. of File to be read: 54
- File Format: parquet
- File Size: Each file of size 40 MB
- No. of cores: 10
- 'minPartitions': Not specified
- 'mapred.min.split.size': (default: 1 MB)
- 'dfs.blocksize': (default: 128 MB)
- 'spark.default.parallelism' (default: Total No. of CPU cores: 10)

Explanation: The number partitions for Example 2.9 comes out as 54. The splitSize for this case also comes out be 128 MB only, so basically, each file has only 1 file chunk since file size is less than the splitSize. Now, since each file chunk maps to single partition, the total partitions come out to be 54.

Example 2.10:

- No. of File to be read: 31
- File Format: parquet
- File Size: Each file of size 330 MB
- No. of cores: 10
- 'minPartitions': 1000
- 'mapred.min.split.size': (default: 1 MB)
- 'dfs.blocksize': (default: 128 MB)
- 'spark.default.parallelism' (default: Total No. of CPU cores: 10)

Explanation: The number partitions for Example 2.10 comes out as 1023. The splitSize for this case comes out be 10.23 MB only, so basically, each file has 33 file chunks since parquet is splittable. Now, since each file chunk maps to single partition, the total partitions come out to be 1023.

Example 2.11:

- No. of File to be read: 31
- File Format: parquet
- File Size: Each file of size 330 MB
- No. of cores: 10
- 'minPartitions': Not specified
- 'mapred.min.split.size': (256 MB)
- 'dfs.blocksize': (default: 128 MB)
- 'spark.default.parallelism' (default: Total No. of CPU cores: 10)

Explanation: The number partitions for Example 2.11 comes out as 62. The splitSize for this case comes out be 256 MB only, so basically, each file has 2 file chunks since parquet is splittable. Now, since each file chunk maps to single partition, the total partitions come out to be 62.

Example 2.12:

- No. of File to be read: 10
- File Format: CSV (compressed with unsplittable compression codec, gzip)
- File Size: Each file of size 355 MB
- No. of cores: 10
- 'minPartitions': Not specified
- 'mapred.min.split.size': (default: 1 MB)
- 'dfs.blocksize': (default: 128 MB)
- 'spark.default.parallelism' (default: Total No. of CPU cores: 10)

Explanation: The number partitions for the Example 2.12 are 10. Each file has only one file chunk since gzip compressed CVS file format is not splittable. Applying the RDD input partitioning rule that each file chunk maps to single partition, the total partitions come out to be 10.

Example 2.13:

- No. of File to be read: 10
- File Format: CSV (compressed with splittable compression codec, bzip2)
- File Size: Each file of size 355 MB
- No. of cores: 10
- 'minPartitions': Not specified
- 'mapred.min.split.size': (default: 1 MB)
- 'dfs.blocksize': (default: 128 MB)
- 'spark.default.parallelism' (default: Total No. of CPU cores: 10)

Explanation: The number partitions for Example 2.13 comes out as 30. The splitSize for this case comes out be 128 MB, so basically, each file has 3 file chunks since CSV with bzip2 compression is splittable. Applying the RDD input partitioning rule that each file chunk maps to single partition, the total partitions come out to be 30.

Example 2.14:

- No. of File to be read: 10
- 'minPartitions': Not specified
- 'mapred.min.split.size' (256 MB)
- 'dfs.blocksize' (default: 128 MB)
- 'spark.default.parallelism' (default: Total No. of CPU cores: 10)

- File Format: CSV (compressed with splittable compression codec, bzip2)
- File Size: Each file of size 355 MB
- No. of cores: 10

Explanation: The number partitions for Example 2.14 comes out as 20. The splitSize for this case comes out be 256 MB, so basically, each file has 2 file chunks since CSV with bzip2 compression is splittable. Applying the RDD input partitioning rule that each file chunk maps to single partition, the total partitions come out to be 20.

Recommendations

After you have looked upon the detailed procedure of deciding the input partitions of a Dataset or an RDD, here are some recommendations on tweaking the input partitions.

- If you are working on a Dataset to read data from a set of splittable data files (without a bucket specification), then by keeping the 'spark.default.parallelism' to 1, you can adjust the value of configuration 'maxPartitionBytes' appropriately to read the desired amount of data per partition. Therefore, if you desire lesser bytes to be read per partitions, the number of input partitions in the Dataset would be more as compared to the case when you desire more bytes to be read per partition. More number of partitions, where each partition reads a lesser number of bytes from the data file(s), is helpful to optimize memory intensive transformations. On the other hand, a smaller number of partitions, where each partition reads comparatively higher number of bytes from the data file(s), is helpful in maximizing the computational productivity for transformations that are not memory intensive.

- If you are working with a Dataset to read data from a set of unsplittable data files (without a bucket specification), then by keeping the 'spark.default.parallelism' to 1, you can tweak the configuration 'maxPartitionBytes' to an appropriate value to read one or multiple data files per partitions. As explained in the partition packing procedure for Datasets, each unsplittable file is one file chunk regardless of the size of the file, therefore, you only have the flexibility of either reading one data file per partition or multiple files per partition by adjusting the value of 'maxPartitionBytes'.

- If you are working on an RDD to read data from a set of splittable data files (without a bucket specification), then you should understand that the baseline size per partition is equal to HDFS block size. If you want to read data greater than the block size bytes for the input RDD partitions, then you could explicitly set "mapred.min.split.size" to an appropriate value greater than the block size while keeping other partitioning parameters at the default values. Also, if you want to read data lesser than the block size bytes for the input RDD partitions, then you should increase the 'minPartitions' to an appropriate value while keeping other partitioning parameters at the default values.

- If you are working on an RDD to read data from a set of unsplittable data files (without a bucket specification), then you can't do anything to adjust the input partitions of the RDD. As explained earlier, each of unsplittable file constitutes one file chunk only irrespective of the file size and since RDD input partitioning scheme always constitutes one partition for one file chunk, the number of partitions is always equal to number of unsplittable data files.

- Partitions are read record wise, meaning, the record reader of the partition would search the partition, right from the start, to find the first beginning byte of a record. Once a beginning of a record is found, the record reader aligns to that and start reading the record. Thereafter, the subsequent records whose beginning lies within the partitions are also read. Based on this fact, therefore, you should not make your input partitions so small that some of the partitions does not even contain a single data record beginning, because then those partitions would be uselessly processed and incur unnecessary computational overhead. *For example*, for parquet file format, a row group forms the record of a parquet and has a default size of 128 MB. Therefore, if you split a large parquet file into partitions with size less than 128 MB, then you would end up with some partitions which would not contain any row group beginning making all those partitions useless for processing.

Input Partitions of a Dataset from a set of Data Files with Bucketing specification

When you specify a Dataset to read a set of Data Files against a bucketing specification, the number of resultant partitions are always equal to the number of partitions specified in the bucketing specification. Bucketing specification, as explained earlier, is stored in the metadata of a table. Therefore, one must read the set of data files by specifying the table either by using the SPARK SQL expression, or by using the table API on a DataFrameReader instance.

```
'sparkSession.read().option(\"path\",#specifiy_path).ta
ble(#specifiy_table)'
```

Each of the data file, splittable or unsplittable, is mapped to only one of the input partitions being decided by the bucketing specification. The mapped partition is always equal to the 'bucketID' extracted from the name of the data file. 'bucketID' is extracted for each of the data file from the corresponding file name by assuming the following format of the file name:

```
<Prefix>_<bucketID>.<Extension>
```

Here is an example for the same representing a snappy compressed parquet file having 'bucketID' equal to 00001.

```
'part-00000-e4730f55-ca8f-4425-b505-
5747f52aadd4_00001.c000.snappy.parquet'
```

When you bucketize your data and write in disk, bucketized data files are produced. These bucketized data files contain the 'bucketID' in the file name.

Chapter 3

Partitioning during Spark Transformations

As you are aware, Spark programs are all about transformations and actions. In a nutshell, a Spark transformation transforms one or more partitioned datasets into an output partitioned dataset. Spark achieves the same by computing the partitions of the output dataset by operating on the data contained in partitions of the input datasets.

Partitioning of the output data set plays a very important role in ensuring the reliability and efficiency of the underlying transformation. Improper partitioning of the output dataset, resulting from a transformation, could also affect the other subsequent transformations down the data pipeline. Therefore, it is important to understand how the partitioning in the output dataset gets affected by the various transformations that are available in Spark.

At a high level, all available Spark transformations are being broadly classified into two main categories. This is based on the computational relationship between partitions of the output dataset and input datasets. The categories are termed as Narrow Transformation and Wide Transformations.

Narrow Transformations

In narrow transformation, each partition of an input dataset is used for computing at most one partition of the output dataset. Meaning, there is either one to one mapping or many to one mapping between input and output partitions as shown in Figure 3.1

The simplest example of narrow transformation is the 'map' transformation which is having one to one relationship between input and output transformation. The other examples of narrow transformations are:

- Filter
- FlatMap
- Union
- Hash-Partitioned Join
- Coalesce

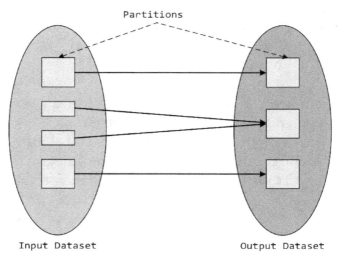

Fig. 3.1: Input and Output Partitions Relationship in Narrow Transformations

Wide Transformations

In Wide transformations, a partition of an input dataset is used for computing multiple partitions of the output dataset. Meaning, there is one to many mappings between input and output partitions in wide transformations.

The easiest to understand example of a wide transformation is aggregation operator where you aggregate data in multiple input partitions to compute an output partition. The other examples are:

- Join
- GroupByKey
- ReduceByKey
- Repartition

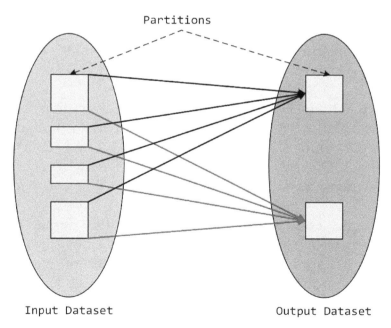

Fig. 3.2: Input and Output Partitions Relationship in Wide
Transformations

Output Partitioning for Spark Transformations

One-to-One Output Partitioning

For a subset of the narrow transformations, the number of output partitions are always equal to the number of input transformations. Each output partition for this subset is computed exclusively from one input partition only. Also, these transformations apply to a single input RDD or Dataset. Examples of such transformations are 'map', 'flatMap', 'filter', 'sample', etc.

Output Partitioning in Union

Union transformation collects data together that is distributed across two or more Datasets or RDDs.

The resultant Dataset/RDD after the execution of union transformation represents the unified data contained in multiple input Datasets/RDDs. The unified data in the resultant Dataset/RDD can then be operated together via subsequent Spark transformations.

Although, you would interpret from the name, that the number of output partitions, after the Union is executed, would be sum of the individual number of partitions of various input Datasets/RDDs, but it is not always like that. Number of Output partitions, after executing a Union transformation, is decided differently in case of RDDs and Datasets:

Union on RDDs:

When you perform a union on two or more RDDs, the number of partitions in the output RDD are chosen using the following rules:

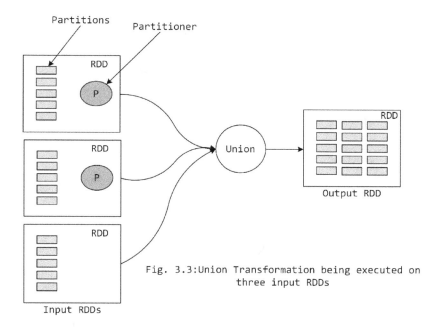

Fig. 3.3:Union Transformation being executed on three input RDDs

- If all the input RDDs have the same Partitioner and equal number of partitions, then the number of partitions in the resultant RDD is same as in each of the input RDD.

- If the input RDDs differ in number of partitions, or have different Partitioners, then the Union transformation adds up the number of partitions in the all the parent RDDs to determine the number of partitions in the output RDD. This is true even when one of the RDD among all the input RDDs possess either different partitioners or different number of partitions as compared to the rest of the lot.

- If the Partitioner is absent in one or more input RDDs, then, also the Union transformation adds up the number of partitions in the parent RDDs to determine the number of partitions in the output RDD. This is true even when all the input RDDs have the same number of partitions.

Let us now see some examples to get clarity on these output partitioning rules. All the examples assume two RDDs 'A' and 'B' taking part in following union transformation to produce a union RDD 'C':

```
C = A.union(B)
```

Example 3.1

- There is a Partitioner P1 of type P which partitions an RDD into 1000 partitions.
- 'A' is re-partitioned by a Partitioner P1.
- 'B' is re-partitioned by a Partitioner P1.

Explanation: The union RDD 'C' for Example 3.1 would have 1000 partitions. This is due to the fact that both RDDs, 'A' and 'B' contains the same partitioner.

Example 3.2

- There is a Partitioner P1 of type P partitioning an RDD into 1000 partitions.
- There is a Partitioner P2 of type P partitioning an RDD into 500 partitions.
- 'A' is re-partitioned by a Partitioner P1.
- 'B' is re-partitioned by a Partitioner P2.

Explanation: The union RDD C for Example 3.2 would have 1500 partitions. Here, although, RDDs 'A' and 'B' contain the same type of partitioner, the number of partitions is different for 'A' and 'B'. Therefore, the union RDD 'C', according to the rules, would have the number of partitions equal to the sum of partitions of 'A' and 'B'.

Example 3.3

- There is a Partitioner P1 of type P partitioning an RDD into 1000 partitions.
- There is a Partitioner Q1 of type Q partitioning an RDD into 1000 partitions.
- 'A' is re-partitioned by a Partitioner P1.
- 'B' is re-partitioned by a Partitioner Q1.

Explanation: The union RDD 'C' for Example 3.3 would have 2000 partitions. Here, RDDs A and B contain the different type of partitioners, although, the number of partitions is equal for 'A' and 'B'. Therefore, the union RDD 'C', according to the rules, would have the number of partitions equal to the sum of partitions of 'A' and 'B'.

Union on Datasets:

Output partitioning is much simplified when you perform Union on multiple Datasets. In the case of union transformation on multiple input Datasets, the number of partitions in the output Dataset is always equal to the sum of the individual number of partitions of all input Datasets.

Output Partitioning in Aggregation

Aggregation transformation aggregates the data across multiple partitions in an RDD or a Dataset, in accordance to chosen aggregation key. An aggregation function, such as 'sum', 'max', etc. can be optionally applied to the aggregated data to transform the aggregated data per aggregation key. The aggregated transformed data is spread across the partitions of the aggregated RDD/Dataset in accordance with aggregation keys. Meaning, the aggregated transformed data for an aggregation key would be available in only one of the partitions of the aggregated RDD/Dataset.

Number of output partitions differs when aggregation is performed on a raw RDD as compared to when aggregation is performed on a Dataset. Below is the description of how the output number of partitions is decided when aggregation is performed over RDD and Dataset:

Aggregation on an RDD

While executing an aggregation transformation on an RDD, you have the flexible option of choosing one of the two flavors of various aggregation APIs. One of the flavors implicitly chooses the number of partitions for the resultant aggregated RDD, while the other one allows a programmer to explicitly mention the number of partitions in the resultant aggregated RDD.

Below are some of the aggregation APIs on RDDs where the output number of partitions are decided implicitly:

- `reduceByKey (scala.Function2<V,V,V> func))`
- `groupByKey ()`

- aggregateByKey (U zeroValue,
  scala.Function2<U,V,U> seqOp, scala.Function2<U,U,U>
  combOp, scala.reflect.ClassTag<U> evidence$2)

For all the three aggregation APIs, another flavor is also provided where the number of output partitions needs to be specified explicitly as the part of the APIs itself. These are:

- reduceByKey (scala.Function2<V,V,V> func, int
  numPartitions)
- groupByKey (int numPartitions)
- aggregateByKey (U zeroValue, int numPartitions,
  scala.Function2<U,V,U> seqOp, scala.Function2<U,U,U>
  combOp, scala.reflect.ClassTag<U> evidence$2)

To determine the output number of partitions in case of implicit APIs, aggregation APIs first lookout for a configuration property 'spark.default.parallelism'. If the

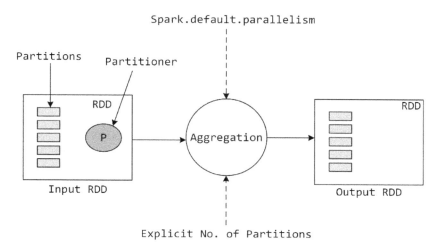

Fig. 3.4: Factors deciding Output partitioning while performing aggregation on an RDD

property is not set, the number of partitions in the aggregated output RDD is always equal to the number of partitions in the input RDD on which the aggregation is performed.

However, if the config property 'spark.default.parallelism' is set to some value, then there are two paths to decide on the number of output partitions in the aggregated RDD:

- If the input RDD has a partitioner on aggregation key, then the number of partitions in the aggregated output RDD is equal to the number of partitions in the input RDD.
- If input RDD does not have a partitioner, then the number of partitions in the aggregated output RDD is equal to the value of 'spark.default.parallelism'.

Let us now see some examples to get clarity on output partitioning rules applicable to the aggregation operation on RDDs. All the examples assume that RDD 'A' is being aggregated to produce the output aggregated RDD 'B':

Example 3.4

- 'A' does not contain any Partitioner.
- Number of partitions in A are 100
- Config 'spark.default.parallelism' is not set explicitly
- Aggregation expression is 'B = A.groupbyKey()'

Explanation: Aggregated Output Dataset 'B' for Example 3.4 would have 100 partitions. This is because, 'A' does not contain any partitioner and the config property 'spark.default.parallelism' is not set explicitly, hence, the number of partitions for the Output Dataset B, according to the rules, would be equal to the input number of partitions which is 100.

Example 3.5

- 'A' does not contain any Partitioner.
- Number of partitions in A are 100
- Config 'spark.default.parallelism' is set to 50.
- Aggregation expression is 'B = A.groupbyKey()'

Explanation: Aggregated Output Dataset 'B' for Example 3.5 would have 50 partitions. This is because, 'A' does not contain any partitioner and the config property 'spark.default.parallelism' is set explicitly to 50, hence, the number of partitions for the Output Dataset B, according to the rules, would be equal to the config value which is 50.

Example 3.6

- 'A' contains a Partitioner portioning the A on 100 partitions
- Config 'spark.default.parallelism' is set to 500
- Aggregation expression is 'B = A.groupbyKey()'

Explanation: Aggregated Output Dataset B for Example 3.5 would have 100 partitions. This is because, 'A' here contains a partitioner and the config property 'spark.default.parallelism' is also set explicitly to 500, but, according to the rules, the partitioner's number of partitions would take precedence and therefore the number of output partitions for the Output Dataset 'B' would be equal to 100.

Example 3.7

- 'A' contains a Partitioner portioning the A on 100 partitions
- Config 'spark.default.parallelism' is set to 500.
- Aggregation expression is 'B = A.groupbyKey(50)'

Explanation: Aggregated Output Dataset B for Example 3.6 would have 50 partitions. This is because, although, 'A' here contains a partitioner and the config property 'spark.default.parallelism' is also set explicitly to 500, but, the number of output partitions are provided explicitly in the aggregation API itself. Therefore, the number of output partitions for the Output Dataset B would be equal to 50.

Aggregation on a Dataset

Aggregation on an input Dataset is executed by specifying a desirable aggregation key made up of one or more attributes/fields of the input Dataset. Following are the two ways in which the number of partitions in the output aggregated Dataset is decided:

- If the input Dataset (to be aggregated) is already partitioned strictly on the basis of either all or subset of the attributes of the aggregation key, then the output aggregated Dataset has the same number of partitions as in the parent Dataset. The input Dataset can already be partitioned in the desirable way due to a previous transformation of repartition, aggregation or join type.

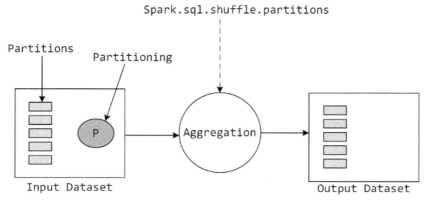

Fig. 3.5:Factors deciding partitioning of an Aggregated Dataset

- If the input Dataset is not already partitioned on the basis of all or subset of the attributes of the aggregation key, then the number of partitions in the output aggregated Dataset is always equal to value of Spark config 'spark.sql.shuffle.partitions', the default value for which is set to 200.

Let us now see some examples to get clarity on output partitioning rules applicable to aggregation operation on Datasets. All the examples assume that Dataset 'A' being aggregated to produce the output aggregated Dataset 'B'.

Here is the schema of Dataset A

```
root:
 | --  empId: Integer
 | --  sal: Integer
 | --  name: String
 | --  address: String
 | --  dept: Integer
```

and, here is the aggregation expression applicable for all the examples.

```
B = A.groupBy(functions.col("empId"),
functions.col("dept")).agg(functions.sum(functions.col("sal"
)));
```

Example 3.8

- 'A' is not partitioned on the aggregation key (empId, dept) earlier
- Number of partitions in A are 100
- Config 'spark.sql.shuffle.partitions' is at default value of 200.

Explanation: Aggregated Output Dataset 'B' for Example 3.8 would have 200 partitions. Since, 'A' is not already partitioned on the aggregation key, the number of partitions for the Output Dataset 'B', according to the rules, would be 200.

Example 3.9

- 'A' is partitioned on the aggregation key (empId, dept).
- Number of partitions in A are 100
- Config 'spark.sql.shuffle.partitions' is explicitly set to a value of 500.

Explanation: Aggregated Output Dataset 'B' for Example 3.9 would have 100 partitions. Since, 'A' is already partitioned on all the attributes of the aggregation key, the number of partitions for the Output Dataset 'B', according to the rules, would be 100.

Example 3.10

- 'A' is partitioned on the aggregation key (dept).
- Number of partitions in A are 100
- Config 'spark.sql.shuffle.partitions' is explicitly set to a value of 500.

Explanation: Aggregated Output Dataset 'B' for Example 3.10 would have 100 partitions. Since, 'A' is already partitioned on one of the attributes of the aggregation key, the number of partitions for the Output Dataset 'B', according to the rules, would be 100.

Example 3.11

- 'A' is partitioned on the key (empId,dept,sal).
- Number of partitions in A are 100
- Config 'spark.sql.shuffle.partitions' is explicitly set to a value of 500.

Explanation: Aggregated Output Dataset 'B' for Example 3.11 would have 500 partitions. Since, 'A' is partitioned on an additional attribute which is missing in the aggregation key, the number of partitions for the Output Dataset 'B', according to the rules, would be 500.

Output Partitioning in Joins

Join transformations are heavily used in Spark applications to correlate two data collections. A Join transformation joins two RDDs or two Datasets on a join condition to produce an output RDD or Dataset. Process of selecting the number of output partitions differs in case when you join two RDDs as compared to the case when you join two Datasets.

Join on RDDs

Join transformations are applicable only on Pair RDDs of type RDD<K,V>. To perform Join operation on Pair RDDs, programmers are being provided with two set of APIs. In one of the two sets, the programmer can explicitly specify either the number of partitions, or the Partitioner. Therefore, for this set, the specified number of partitions, or the number of partitions contained in the specified Partitioner directly becomes the number of partitions in the resultant joined RDD.

Here are some of the Joins APIs from the explicit set which are available on a Pair RDD 'A':

- `A.join(RDD<scala.Tuple2<K,W>> other, int numPartitions)`
- `A.leftOuterJoin(RDD<scala.Tuple2<K,W>> other, int numPartitions)`
- `A.rightOuterJoin(RDD<scala.Tuple2<K,W>> other, int numPartitions)`
- `A.fullOuterJoin(RDD<scala.Tuple2<K,W>> other, int numPartitions)`
- `A.join(RDD<scala.Tuple2<K,W>> other, Partitioner partitioner)`
- `A.leftOuterJoin(RDD<scala.Tuple2<K,W>> other, Partitioner partitioner)`

- `A.rightOuterJoin(RDD<scala.Tuple2<K,W>> other, Partitioner partitioner)`
- `A.fullOuterJoin(RDD<scala.Tuple2<K,W>> other, Partitioner partitioner)`

In the other set, the programmer neither specifies the number of partitions nor any Partitioner explicitly in the Join APIs. Spark chooses the number of output partitions of the Joined RDD itself.

Here are some of the Joins APIs from the implicit set which are available on a Pair RDD 'A':

- `A.join(RDD<scala.Tuple2<K,W>> other)`
- `A.leftOuterJoin(RDD<scala.Tuple2<K,W>> other)`
- `A.rightOuterJoin(RDD<scala.Tuple2<K,W>> other)`
- `A.fullOuterJoin(RDD<scala.Tuple2<K,W>> other)`

Following are the rules in which the number of partitions in the resultant joined RDD is decided for implicit set:

- If no input Pair RDD (participating in join operation) has a partitioner on the associated Key, then the number of partitions in the output joined RDD is equal to the value configured for the config property 'spark.default.parallelism'. However, if this config property is not set to any value, then the number of partitions in the output joined RDD is equal to the maximum of the number of partitions of input RDDs. (The above-described behavior is same across old and recent Spark versions)

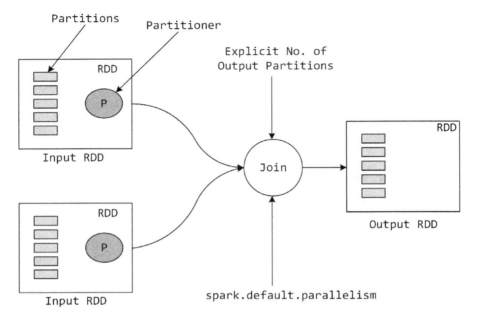

Fig. 3.6: Factors deciding partitioning of a Joined RDD

- If one or both input RDDs have a partitioner on the Key, then the maximum value of the number of partitions among the partitioner owning input RDDs is compared with config property 'spark.default.parallelism' in the following ways (in accordance with the latest versions of Spark) to choose the number of output partitions in the output joined RDD:

  o If the config property is set to some value, and the maximum value is above the config value, then the maximum value is chosen as the number of partitions in the output joined RDD.

o   If the config property is set to some value and the maximum value is below that value, but, the maximum value is within a single order of magnitude of the config value, then the maximum value is chosen as the number of partitions in the output joined RDD.

o   If the config property is set to some value and the maximum value is below that value, but, the maximum value is not within a single order of magnitude of the highest number of partitions among input RDDs, then config property value is chosen as the number of partitions in the output joined RDD.

o   If the config property is not set, then the maximum value is chosen as the number of partitions in the output joined RDD.

Note: In older versions of Spark, if either one or both parent Pair RDDs have partitioner on the Key object, then the maximum of number of partitions among partitioner contained input RDDs is always chosen as the number of partitions for the output joined RDD irrespective of the value being set for the config property, 'spark.default.parallelism'

Let us see the few examples to concretize the various aspects of the rules applicable for deciding the output partitions on two Pair RDDs namely 'RDD1' and 'RDD2' for the following Join expression:

```
RDD3 = RDD1.join(RDD2)
```

Example 3.12

- Configuration 'spark.default.parallelism' not set.
- 'RDD1' have 20 partitions but does not contain a Partitioner
- 'RDD2' have 10 partitions but does not contain a Partitioner

Explanation: Joined RDD, 'RDD3', for Example 3.12 would have 20 partitions. 'RDD1' and 'RDD2' does not contain partitioner and the configuration 'spark.default.parallelism' is not set to any value, therefore maximum of number of partitions for 'RDD1' and 'RDD2' which comes out to be 20 is chosen as the number of partitions for the joined RDD, 'RDD3', according to rules.

Example 3.13

- Configuration 'spark.default.parallelism' is set to 5.
- 'RDD1' have 20 partitions but does not contain a Partitioner
- 'RDD2' have 10 partitions but does not contain a Partitioner

Explanation: Joined RDD, 'RDD3', for Example 3.13 would have 5 partitions. 'RDD1' and 'RDD2' does not contain partitioner but the configuration 'spark.default.parallelism' is set to 5 explicitly in this example, therefore irrespective of the fact that the config value is lesser than the number of partitions of either 'RDD1' and 'RDD2', the config value would be chosen as the number of partitions for the joined RDD, 'RDD3', according to rules

Example 3.14

- Configuration 'spark.default.parallelism' is set to 500.
- 'RDD1' already re-partitioned using a Partitioner P1, and have 1000 partitions
- 'RDD2' have 1500 partitions but does not contain a Partitioner

Explanation: Joined RDD, 'RDD3', for Example 3.14 would have 1000 partitions. In this example, only RDD1 contains a partitioner and the configuration 'spark.default.parallelism' is also set to 500 explicitly. Also, number of partitions for the partitioner contained in 'RDD1' is greater than the config 'spark.default.parallelism' . Hence, number of partitions of 'RDD1' would also be chosen as the number of partitions for the joined RDD, 'RDD3', according to rules.

Example 3.15

- Configuration 'spark.default.parallelism' is set to 500.
- 'RDD1' is repartitioned using a Partitioner P1, and have 1000 partitions
- 'RDD2' is repartitioned using a Partitioner P1, and have 1500 partitions

Explanation: Joined RDD, 'RDD3', for Example 3.15 would have 1500 partitions. In this example, both 'RDD1' and 'RDD2' contains a partitioner and the configuration 'spark.default.parallelism' is set to 500 explicitly. Therefore, according to the rules, the maximum of number of partitions for 'RDD1' and 'RDD2' would be compared against the config value for 'spark.default.parallelism' . Since, the number of partitions of 'RDD2' are more than 'RDD1' and the config value, hence, that would also be chosen as the number of partitions for the joined RDD, 'RDD3'.

Example 3.16

- Configuration 'spark.default.parallelism' is set to 1500.
- 'RDD1' already re-partitioned using a Partitioner P1, and have 1000 partitions
- 'RDD2' already re-partitioned using a Partitioner P1, and have 1000 partitions

Explanation: Joined RDD, 'RDD3', for Example 3.16 would have 1000 partitions. In this example, 'RDD1' and 'RDD2' contains a partitioner and the configuration 'spark.default.parallelism' is set to 1500 explicitly. Therefore, according to the rules, the maximum of number of partitions for 'RDD1' and 'RDD2' would be compared against the config value for 'spark.default.parallelism' . Since, the maximum value, 1000, is within a single order of magnitude of the config value, therefore, 1000 would be chosen as the number of partitions for the joined RDD, 'RDD3'.

Example 3.17

- Configuration 'spark.default.parallelism' is set to 1500.
- 'RDD1' already re-partitioned using a Partitioner P1, and have 10 partitions
- 'RDD2' already re-partitioned using a Partitioner P1, and have 12 partitions

Explanation: Joined RDD, 'RDD3', for Example 3.16 would have 1500 partitions. In this example, both, 'RDD1' and 'RDD2' contains a partitioner and the configuration 'spark.default.parallelism' is set to 1500 explicitly. Therefore, according to the rules, the maximum of number of partitions for 'RDD1' and 'RDD2' would be compared against the config value for 'spark.default.parallelism' . Since, the maximum value, 12, is not within a single order of magnitude of the config value, therefore, the config value which is 1500 would be chosen as the number of partitions for the joined RDD, 'RDD3'.

Join on Datasets

Join on Datasets is much more comprehensive. Join APIs for Datasets do not allow programmers to explicitly mention the number of partitions as in case of RDDs. Spark always determine the resultant number of partitions in the Joined Dataset by itself. Output partitioning in Join transformations for Datasets depends on the following factors:

- Physical mechanism adopted by Spark to execute a particular Join operation
- Output Partitioning structure of the input Datasets
- Value of the config property, 'spark.sql.shuffle.partitions'

There are the five types of Join mechanisms out of which Spark selects the one to finally execute the Join (rules governing the selection are out of scope of this chapter):

- Broadcast Hash Join
- Shuffle Hash Join
- Sort Merge Join
- Cartesian Join
- Broadcast Nested Loop Join

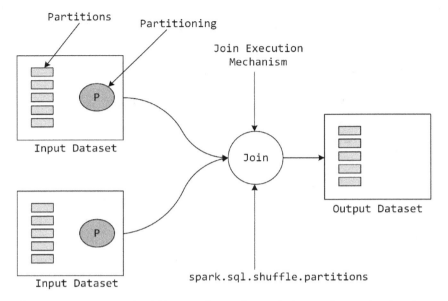

Fig. 3.7: Factors deciding number of partitions of a Joined Dataset

Let us see how the output partitioning of the output Dataset is decided for each of the Join mechanism. We would also see examples for each of the mechanism where two Datasets namely 'DS1' and 'DS2' are joined to produce 'DS3'. Both the Datasets have the following similar schema:

```
root:
 |  --   empId: Integer
 |  --   sal: Integer
 |  --   name: String
 |  --   address: String
 |  --   dept: Integer
```

Broadcast Hash Join

In Broadcast Hash Join mechanism, one of the two input Datasets (participating in the Join) is broadcasted to all the executors. A Hash Table is being built on all the executors from the broadcasted Dataset, after which, each partition of the non-broadcasted input Dataset is joined independently to the other Dataset being available as a local hash table.

It must be obvious from the functioning of Broadcast Hash Join that the number of output partitions of the resultant Dataset is always equal to the number of partitions of the non-broadcasted input Dataset.

Example 3.18

- Let's say, following is the Join expression for 'DS3'
- DS3 = DS1.join(DS2
    ,DS1.col("empId").equalTo(DS2.col("empId")))
    .select(DS1.col("empId"),DS2.col("sal")
    ,DS2.col("dept"));
- 'DS2' has 100 partitions and is broadcasted to all executors.
- 'DS1' has 50 partitions

Explanation: The number of partitions of the output Dataset 'DS3' for Example would be equal to number of partitions of the input Dataset 'DS1', i.e. 50, since 'DS1' is not broadcasted.

Shuffle Hash Join, Sort Merge Join

In both, Shuffle Hash Join and Sort Merge Join, firstly output partitioning with a certain number of output partitions is decided. Then, Spark ensures that both the input Datasets are aligned to the selected output partitioning. If one or both of them are not aligned, then a shuffle operation is executed (before the Join operation) to align the unaligned input Dataset(s).

After the conformance to the selected output partitioning is ensured for both the input Datasets, the further execution path of the two join approaches gets different. Shuffle Hash executes the Join operation per output partition using the standard Hash Join approach. The Hash table (being used in the Hash Join approach) is being built on the data which belongs to the smaller input Dataset.

On the other hand, Sort Merge executes the Join operation per output partition using the standard Sort Merge Join approach. Data belonging to both the input Datasets mapped to an output partition is first sorted in accordance with the identified Join Key(s), the sorted Datasets are then merged according to the Join procedure to produce the resultant Joined data.

Let us now see the rules deciding he output partitions of the Joined Dataset is decided for the Shuffle Hash and Sort Merge Join:

- If none of the two input Datasets (participating in the Join transformation) is already hash partitioned on the respective Join Key(s), then the configured value of 'spark.sql.shuffle.partitions' is chosen as the number of partitions in the output joined Dataset.
- If one or both of the input Datasets are already hash partitioned based on respective Join Key(s), then the maximum value of the number of partitions among these input RDDs is compared against the configured value of 'spark.sql.shuffle.partitions' in the following ways to decide on the resultant number of partitions:
    - If the maximum value is above the configured value of 'spark.sql.shuffle.partitions', then the

maximum value is chosen as the number of partitions in the output joined Dataset.

- o If the maximum value is below the configured value of 'spark.sql.shuffle.partitions', then the configured value is chosen as the number of partitions in the output joined Dataset.

Here are some examples for Shuffle Hash Join and Broadcast Join based on the following join expression for 'DS3':

```
DS3 = DS1.join(DS2,
        DS1.col("empId").equalTo(DS2.col("empId"))
        .and(DS1.col("name").equalTo(DS2.col("name")))
        .and(DS1.col("address").equalTo(DS2.col("address"))))
        .select(DS1.col("empId"),DS2.col("sal"),DS2.col("dept"));
```

Example 3.19

- 'DS1' is not hash partitioned and have 500 partitions.
- 'DS2' is not hash partitioned and have 100 partitions.
- Config property, 'spark.sql.shuffle.partitions', set to 200 (default)

Explanation: The number of partitions of the output Dataset DS3 for Example 3.19 would be equal to config value of 'spark.sql.shuffle.partitions', i.e., 200. This is because, here, DS1 and DS2 both are not hash partitioned. Therefore, according to rules, config value 700 of 'spark.sql.shuffle.partitions' would be selected as the number of output partitions for the joined dataset DS3.

Example 3.20

- 'DS1' already hash partitioned on the Join Key ('empId','name','address') on 500 partitions.
- 'DS2' already hash partitioned on the Join Key ('empId','name','address') on 100 partitions.
- Config property, 'spark.sql.shuffle.partitions', set to 200 (default)

Explanation: The number of partitions of the output Dataset 'DS3' for Example 3.20 would be equal to partitions of 'DS1', i.e. 500. This is because, both 'DS1' and 'DS2' are already hash partitioned on respective Join Keys, and also, the maximum of the number of partitions of 'DS1' and 'DS2', 500, is greater than the config value 200 of 'spark.sql.shuffle.partitions'. Therefore, according to rules, 500 would be selected as the number of output partitions for the joined dataset 'DS3'.

Example 3.21

- 'DS1' already hash partitioned on the Join Key ('empId','name','address') on 500 partitions.
- 'DS2' already hash partitioned on the Join Key ('empId','name','address') on 100 partitions.
- Config property, 'spark.sql.shuffle.partitions', set to 700.

Explanation: The number of partitions of the output Dataset 'DS3' for Example 3.21 would be equal to config value of 'spark.sql.shuffle.partitions', i.e., 700. This is because, although, both 'DS1' and 'DS2' are already hash partitioned on respective Join Keys, but, the maximum of the number of partitions of 'DS1' and 'DS2', 500, is lesser than the config value 700 of 'spark.sql.shuffle.partitions'. Therefore, according to rules, 700 would be selected as the number of output partitions for the joined dataset 'DS3'.

Example 3.22

- 'DS1' already hash partitioned on the Join Key ('empId','name','address') on 500 partitions.
- 'DS2' not already hash partitioned and have 100 partitions.
- Config property, 'spark.sql.shuffle.partitions', set to 200.

Explanation: The number of partitions of the output Dataset 'DS3' for Example 3.22 would be equal to partitions of 'DS1', i.e. 500. This is because, here, only 'DS1' is hash partitioned on the respective Join Key and the number of partitions of the 'DS1' is also greater the config value 200 of 'spark.sql.shuffle.partitions'. Therefore, according to rules, 500 would be selected as the number of output partitions for the joined dataset 'DS3'.

Example 3.23

- 'DS1' already hash partitioned on ('empId') on 500 partitions.
- 'DS2' not hash partitioned and have 100 partitions.
- Config property, 'spark.sql.shuffle.partitions', set to 700.

Explanation: The number of partitions of the output Dataset DS3 for Example 3.23 would be equal to config value of 'spark.sql.shuffle.partitions', i.e., 700. This is because, 'DS1' although hash partitioned, it is not partitioned on the respective Join Key. Further, 'DS2' is not hash partitioned. Therefore, according to rules, config value 700 of 'spark.sql.shuffle.partitions' would be selected as the number of output partitions for the joined dataset 'DS3'.

Cartesian Join

In Cartesian Join, the number of partitions in the output Joined Dataset is always equal to the product of number of partitions of the input Datasets. For each of the output partition of the output Dataset, the data is computed by doing a cartesian product on data from two input partitions, one belonging to one of the input Datasets and the other belonging to the other input dataset.

Let see an example to understand the output partitioning in case of a Cartesian Join executed in context of the following expression:

Example 3.24

```
DS3 = DS1.join(DS2,
      DS1.col("empId").equalTo(DS2.col("empId"))
      .or(DS1.col("name").equalTo(DS2.col("name"))))
      .select(DS1.col("empId"),DS2.col("sal"),DS2.col("dept"));
```

- 'DS1' has 100 partitions.
- 'DS2' has 100 partitions

Explanation: The number of partitions of the output Dataset 'DS3' for Example 3.24 would be equal to product of number of partitions of the input Datasets 'DS1' and 'DS2', i.e. 10000.

Broadcast Nested Loop Join

In Broadcast Nested Loop Join, one of the input Dataset is broadcasted to all the executors. After which, each partition of the non-broadcasted input Dataset is joined to the broadcasted Dataset using the standard Nested Loop Join procedure to produce the output joined data.

It must be obvious here also that the number of output partitions of the resultant Dataset is always equal to number of partitions of the non-broadcasted input Dataset.

Let see an example to understand the output partitioning in case of a Broadcast Nested Loop Join executed in context of the following expression:

Example 3.25

```
DS3 = DS1.join( DS2,
           DS1.col("empId").equalTo(DS2.col("empId"))
           .or(DS1.col("name").equalTo(DS2.col("name"))),"leftouter")
           .select(DS1.col("empId"),DS1.col("sal"));
```

- 'DS1' has 100 partitions
- 'DS1' is broadcasted to all executors
- 'DS2' has 1000 partitions

Explanation: The number of partitions of the output Dataset 'DS3' for Example 3.25 would be equal to the number of partitions of 'DS2', i.e., 1000. This is because 'DS2' is not broadcasted.

Chapter 4

Repartition and Coalesce

Repartition and Coalesce are the explicit partitioning APIs that are available to developers for changing the partitioning structure of a Dataset or RDD. These APIs comes handy in the following situations:

Scaling up the computational parallelism

In Spark, a computing task is bound to a data partition and therefore the number of partitions determines the computational parallelism. Therefore, in scenarios, where you have a large number of computing resources (CPUs and Memory) at your disposal, but the Spark computation on a Spark Dataset is not utilizing these effectively, scaling up partitions would allow you to maximize the usage of the available resources which in turn would increase the computational efficiency.

Scaling down the scheduling overhead

In Spark, each stage is composed of multiple computing tasks that are scheduled for execution by the Task scheduler in the Spark driver (of a Spark application). Therefore, if you have a large number of computing tasks (each task corresponding to one data partition) in comparison to available computing resources, the scheduling overhead could contribute a major portion of a task computing time. The increased scheduling overhead when summed up across all the tasks of a stage could eat up the significant portion of overall stage computation time thereby bringing down the overall stage computational efficiency. To address such scenarios, you can appropriately scale down the number of partitions explicitly.

Scaling down the splits of an Output file

The number of partitions directly governs the number of splits written for an output splittable file (such as parquet file) by a Spark application during execution. Usually, a Dataset or RDD to be written into a file would write a similar number of split files as the number of corresponding partitions.

A very large number of written splits against a file, with split files having sizes in range of KBs or few MBs, could take up a significant amount of meta space in a filesystem. To address such scenarios, again you can appropriately scale down the number of partitions explicitly.

Scaling down the memory requirements

In the case of transformations and actions, such as 'mapPartitions' and 'foreachPartition', processing bigger partitions might require more memory per executor in some scenarios. However, if additional memory for each executor cannot be provisioned, one can appropriately increase the number of partitions explicitly to reduce the amount of data in each of the partitions.

Scaling down the disk spills

In case of transformations, such as aggregation, processing bigger partitions often leads to an increased amount of disk spills on the map side of the transformation. Too much disk spill per partition reduces the computational efficiency of the transformation. In addition, disk spilling might require additional memory to be provisioned on the executor as compared to the case without disk spills. To reduce the disk spills, you can appropriately increase the number of partitions explicitly.

Restructure the partitions with respect to key

There may be cases where a Spark Dataset needs to be repartitioned in a certain way before being used as an input to multiple transformations a Spark application. Therefore, it is prudent to explicitly repartition the Spark Dataset in the required manner once and then use the repartitioned Dataset across multiple transformations.

To enable the repeated usage, the repartitioned Dataset can be cached in memory or disk using persist APIs exposed by the Spark. The repartitioning in such scenarios is often performed with respect to a key evaluated from one or more fields of a data record contained in a partition.

Assistance to bucketBy

'bucketBy' is a DataFrameWriter API used to bucket-wise write a Spark Dataset. Two important parameters for the 'bucketBy' API are the number of buckets and one or more bucketing columns. Bucketing columns are identified from a data record belonging to the Dataset. 'bucketBy' operation is extensively used to store data in partitioned Hive tables. 'bucketBy' can be extremely slow for large Datasets if partitions are randomly arranged with respect to bucketing columns.

Therefore, often explicit repartitioning is performed on the Dataset before a 'bucketBy' is executed on the same. The repartitioning is usually done with number of output partitions equal to number of buckets and repartitioning key made up of bucketing columns.

Repartition APIs

Various flavors of repartition APIs are used to either increase or decrease the number of partitions of an input Dataset or RDD. The number of partitions in the output repartitioned Dataset are either explicitly or implicitly specified in the APIs. In addition, some of the repartition APIs also allows you to specify how the partitioning shall be executed.

Repartition APIs for Datasets

There are multiple repartition APIs that are available for Datasets. These APIs difference with one another in following aspects:

- Implicit or explicit specification of number of partitions in the output repartitioned Dataset.
- Specification of one or more partitioning expressions, where each partitioning expression is made up of one or more columns of the input Dataset.
- Partitioning methodology which is based on either hash partitioning or range partitioning when one or more partitioning expressions are specified.

The simplest and widely used repartition API just asks for the number of partitions for the output repartitioned Dataset:

```
Dataset<T> B = A.repartition( int numPartitions)
```

The output Dataset 'B' is of the same type T as the input one. Another repartition API being widely used is the following:

```
Dataset<T> B = A.repartition ( int numPartitions,
Column... partitionExprs)
```

This flavor, in addition to asking for the number of partitions in the output repartitioned Dataset, also asks for one or more partitioning expressions. The partitioning expressions are used to hash partition the Dataset 'A'.

`A.repartition (Column... partitionExprs)`	Repartitions the Dataset 'A' by the specified partitioning expressions using hash partitioning approach, the number of output partitions being implicitly specified by the config property 'spark.sql.shuffle.partitions'
`A.repartitionByRange (Column... partitionExprs)`	Repartitions the Dataset 'A' by the specified partitioning expressions using range partitioning approach, the number of output partitions being implicitly specified by the config property 'spark.sql.shuffle.partitions'
`A.repartitionByRange ( int numPartitions, Column... partitionExprs)`	Repartitions the Dataset 'A' by the specified partitioning expressions using range partitioning approach, the number of output partitions are also specified explicitly in the API.

Repartition APIs for RDDs:

There are primarily two APIs that are available to perform explicit repartitioning in case of RDDs. The first one is applicable to any RDD of type T, while the other one is applicable to only Pair RDDs of type (K,V).

Generic repartition API applicable to any RDD 'A' of type T is following:

```
RDD<T> B = A.repartition (int numPartitions)
```

The API only asks for the number of partitions for the output repartitioned Dataset. The output RDD 'B' is of the same type T as the input one.

The other repartitioning API that is application to Pair RDDs of type (K,V) is the following:

```
RDD<K,V> B = A.partitionBy ( Partitioner partitioner)
```

This API gives you full flexibility in controlling the partitioning structure of the output RDD since it directly asks for the custom partitioner object. One can define a custom partitioner by extending the Spark Partitioner class and overriding the two key methods 'getPartition' and 'numPartitions'.

Here is an example of custom partitioner, 'MyCustomPartitioner' defined as following:

```java
import org.apache.spark.Partitioner;
public class MyCustomPartitioner extends Partitioner
{
  private int numParts;
  public MyCustomPartitioner(int numPartitions)
  {
   numParts = numPartitions;
  }
  @Override
  public int numPartitions()
  {
   return numParts;
  }
  @Override
  public int getPartition(Object key)
  {
  /* partition based on the first character of the key you can have your logic here !! */
  return ((String) key).charAt(0) % numParts;
  }
  @Override
  public boolean equals(Object obj)
  {
  if (obj instanceof MyCustomPartitioner)
    {
    MyCustomPartitioner partitionerObject  = (MyCustomPartitioner) obj;
    if (partitionerObject.numParts == this.numParts)
    return true;
    }
    return false;
  }
}
```

Repartition APIs Operation

Repartition APIs perform a wide transformation involving a shuffle operation to repartition a Dataset or RDD. Since, a shuffle operation is involved, there would be shuffle write operation accompanied by a corresponding shuffle read operation whenever a repartition is invoked.

A data record in an input partition is assigned to an output partition according to the partitioning strategy invoked by the repartitioning API. Use of wide transformation enables repartition APIs to either increase or decrease the partitions to any value in the output repartitioned Dataset or RDD.

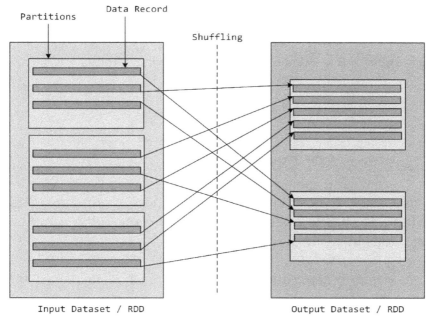

Fig. 4.1: Illustration of Repartition Operation

Coalesce APIs

There is only one coalesce API available for Dataset and one for RDD. This API allows you to explicitly decrease the number of partitions of a Dataset or RDD.

Coalesce API for Dataset

Following is the Coalesce API applicable for a Dataset 'A' of type T. It only asks for the number of output partitions.

```
Dataset<T> B = A.coalesce(int numPartitions)
```

Coalesce API for RDD

Following is the Coalesce API applicable for an RDD 'A' of type T. It also only asks for the number of output partitions.

```
Dataset<T> B = A.coalesce(int numPartitions)
```

Coalesce API Operation

Coalesce API execution involves a narrow transformation, without a shuffle operation, to only decrease the number of partitions in a Dataset or RDD.

In contrast to repartition APIs where each data record in an input partition is assigned to an output partition based on a partitioning strategy, coalesce works at the partition level. In Coalesce, one or more partitions of input Dataset/RDD are mapped to at most single partition of the output Dataset/RDD. Therefore, in coalesce the output number of partitions are always less than or equal to input number of partitions. Also, the mapping strategy of input partitions to an output partition is internal to spark.

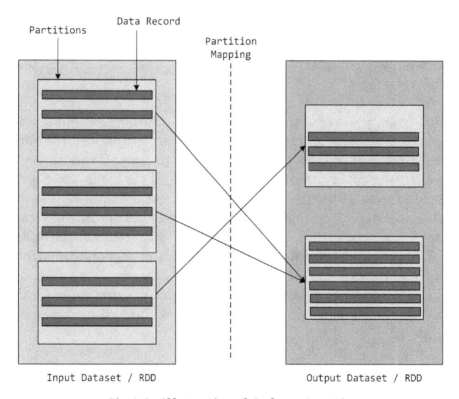

Fig 4.2: Illustration of Coalesce Operation

Repartition or Coalesce

With repartition APIs, you can increase or decrease the number of partitions in a Dataset or RDD, while with Coalesce you can only decrease the number of partitions. Repartition

APIs allows you to control the assignment of data records (in the input partitions) to the output partitions whereas coalesce API do not provide such flexibility on per data record basis.

Further, being a wide transformation, repartition APIs includes a shuffle operation to produce the output partitions. Therefore, repartition APIs bring additional computational overhead to the ongoing Spark Job execution. But, Coalesce API do not include a shuffle operation and hence no additional computational overhead is associated with Coalesce.

However, you need to take care of one important point with Coalesce. Coalesce, being a narrow transformation, it shares the stage computation with the upstream transformations (on the upstream Datasets or RDDs) until a stage barrier is encountered in the upstream RDD DAG of the Spark Job.

This sharing of the stage reduces the parallelism of the whole stage in proportion to the reduced number of partitions specified in the Coalesce API. Therefore, if you drastically reduce the number of partitions with coalesce, it would also drastically hit the parallelism of the transformations on the upstream Datasets or RDDs that share the same stage with coalesce.

On the other hand, repartition, being a wide transformation, the computations on the repartitioned partitions happens in separate stage and therefore it does not affect the parallelism of the upstream transformations (on the upstream Datasets or RDDs).

Here is an example illustrating the parallelism reduction on upstream Datasets due to coalesce operation:

```java
public class SparkCoalesceExample implements Serializable
{
  public static void main(String[] args)
  {
    SparkConf conf = new SparkConf().setMaster("yarn-cluster");

    SparkSession sparkSession
      = SparkSession.builder().config (conf).appName
        ("SparkPartitionerExample").getOrCreate();

    String inputHDFSPath = "/user/poc/data/input_par_83M";

    Dataset<Employee> inputDS
      = sparkSession.sqlContext().parquet File(inputHDFSPath)
                          .as(Encoders.bean(Employee.class))

    inputDS = inputDS.repartition(1000);

    Dataset<Employee> mapSalBolnusDS
      = inputDS.map(((MapFunction<Employee, Employee>) employee ->
              {
                 employee.setSal(employee.getSal() + 2500);
                 return employee;
              }), Encoders.bean(Employee.class));

    mapSalBolnusDS = mapSalBolnusDS.coalesce(50);

    Dataset<Row> deptAggDS
      = mapSalBolnusDS.groupBy(functions.col("deptNo"))
        .agg(functions.sum(functions.col("sal")).as("SumSal"));

    deptAggDS.write().mode(SaveMode.Overwrite)
    .parquet("/user/poc/output/coalesce");
  }
}
```

In the above example, you would expect that map operation on 'inputDS' (producing the Dataset 'mapSalBolnusDS') would execute with 1000 partitions. However, due to the Coalesce on 'mapSalBolnusDS' (after the map operation), the parallelism for map operation is effectively reduced to only 50 from 1000. Therefore, coalesce should be used carefully so that it does not reduce the computational parallelism unwantedly.

Chapter 5
Partitioning to Output Files

Spark applications often persist their intermediate and/or final data sets (represented either by RDDs or Datasets) on the permanent storage medium (such as disk) via a desirable file system, such as HDFS, ext3 (Linux), etc.

If you go by the traditional approach, then firstly you need to collect all the data of the data set (contained in its various partitions) at the driver, and then it can be written into a single file using the traditional filesystem write APIs.

However, for a large data set, the approach would be less reliable and inefficient since, firstly, a large amount of data would require to be transferred over the network to the driver, and secondly, the driver has to fit all this data in its memory until it is written serially into the designed storage backed file. Also, the traditional approach does not provide any opportunity to Spark to optimize the reading process from a traditional single large file.

Therefore, Spark has provided various other options to write a partitioned RDD/Dataset on to storage medium. All these options provide higher reliability and efficiency of the write process as compared to the traditional approach, because all these options rely on per partition writer which writes a subset of partition or the partition as a whole in single storage backed file, termed as part file. These options differ, however, in the way a subset of the partition or the partition as a whole is mapped to a single storage backed file. Various ways provide different optimization opportunities in certain scenarios of reading the data back for subsequent processing.

Basic Approach

The most basic approach that is adopted in Spark to write an RDD/Dataset on a filesystem is to write each partition of the RDD/Dataset in to a separate part file. All the part files, belonging to the same RDD/Dataset, are written in a common directory. The directory is created on the filesystem at the path specified in the corresponding writer API.

This approach ensures a higher write throughput because multiple partitions can be written in parallel if the corresponding computing resources are available to the application.

Here is an example illustrating the approach for a Dataset 'A':

Example 5.1

Dataset 'A' is repartitioned into 10 partitions. 'A' is then written to snappy compressed parquet format at a specified path using the defaults construct for writer API:

```
A = A.repartition(10)
A.write().mode(SaveMode.Overwrite).parquet("/user/poc/e
xample5dot1");
```

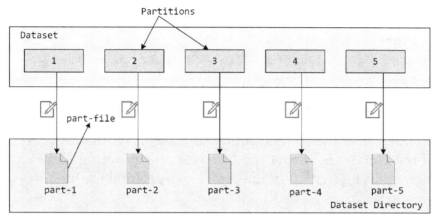

Fig. 5.1: Illustration of the Basic Approach to write
a Dataset on a storage medium such as disk

Executing example 5.1 would create a directory in the filesystem, `example5dot1,` at the specified path. Listing the files in the directory would list 10 part files

- `part-00000-aabcff3c-22f6-4e89-beba-d6d6f7fbe53c-c000.snappy.parquet`
- `part-00001-aabcff3c-22f6-4e89-beba-d6d6f7fbe53c-c000.snappy.parquet`
- `part-00002-aabcff3c-22f6-4e89-beba-d6d6f7fbe53c-c000.snappy.parquet`
- `part-00003-aabcff3c-22f6-4e89-beba-d6d6f7fbe53c-c000.snappy.parquet`
- `part-00004-aabcff3c-22f6-4e89-beba-d6d6f7fbe53c-c000.snappy.parquet`
- `part-00005-aabcff3c-22f6-4e89-beba-d6d6f7fbe53c-c000.snappy.parquet`
- `part-00006-aabcff3c-22f6-4e89-beba-d6d6f7fbe53c-c000.snappy.parquet`

- `part-00007-aabcff3c-22f6-4e89-beba-d6d6f7fbe53c-c000.snappy.parquet`
- `part-00008-aabcff3c-22f6-4e89-beba-d6d6f7fbe53c-c000.snappy.parquet`
- `part-00009-aabcff3c-22f6-4e89-beba-d6d6f7fbe53c-c000.snappy.parquet`

As you can see, each of the part file name carries the partition number after the 'part' prefix. In case, a particular partition in the Dataset is empty then also a corresponding empty part file would be created in the directory specified for the Dataset.

PartitionBy Approach

In this approach, which is only applicable to only Datasets, an additional 'partitionBy' expression is also specified in the writer API. Usually, the expression consists of one or more data fields of the Dataset schema. While writing the data records in a partition, for each of the records, firstly a sub-directory is identified based on the value of 'partitionBy; expression evaluated for the record. The sub-directory has to be present within the primary directory being specified for the Dataset in the writer API. If the identified sub-directory is not present, then the same is created first. Eventually, the data record is written in the partition corresponding file within the identified sub-directory.

Example 5.2
Dataset 'A' is repartitioned into 2 partitions. Also, 'A' has the following schema:

```
root:
|  --   empId: Integer
|  --   sal: Integer
```

```
| --   name: String
| --   address: String
| --   dept: Integer
```

A is then written to a snappy compressed parquet file using the partitionBy clause on 'dept' in the writer API.

```
A = A.repartition(2)

A.write().mode(SaveMode.Overwrite).
.partitionBy("dept").parquet("/user/poc/example5dot2")
```

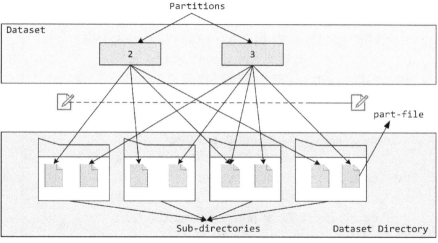

Fig. 5.2: Illustration of using partitionBy approach to write a Dataset on a storage medium

Executing example 5.2 would create a directory example5dot1 at the specified path. Listing the files in the directory would list 5 sub-directories, since the total number unique 'dept' values across all partitions are 5. In each of the sub directory, a file from the each of the partition would be created which would contain all those records from the partition which have corresponding 'dept' value equal to the sub-directory name. If there are no records corresponding to a 'dept' value in a particular partition, then it would not create a file in the corresponding sub-directory.

- dept=101/part-00000-6392f096-3522-4881-8689-cbe9fed2dbe6.c000.snappy.parquet
- dept=101/part-00001-6392f096-3522-4881-8689-cbe9fed2dbe6.c000.snappy.parquet
- dept=102/part-00000-6392f096-3522-4881-8689-cbe9fed2dbe6.c000.snappy.parquet
- dept=102/part-00001-6392f096-3522-4881-8689-cbe9fed2dbe6.c000.snappy.parquet
- dept=103/part-00000-6392f096-3522-4881-8689-cbe9fed2dbe6.c000.snappy.parquet
- dept=103/part-00001-6392f096-3522-4881-8689-cbe9fed2dbe6.c000.snappy.parquet
- dept=104/part-00000-6392f096-3522-4881-8689-cbe9fed2dbe6.c000.snappy.parquet
- dept=104/part-00001-6392f096-3522-4881-8689-cbe9fed2dbe6.c000.snappy.parquet
- dept=105/part-00000-6392f096-3522-4881-8689-cbe9fed2dbe6.c000.snappy.parquet
- dept=105/part-00001-6392f096-3522-4881-8689-cbe9fed2dbe6.c000.snappy.parquet

As you can see, for example 5.2, there are 5 unique values of dept across all partitions. Further, each of the partition contains all the 5 unique values among its records. Therefore, there would be 5 sub-directories would be created, and each of the sub-directory would contain 2 files each corresponding to 2 partitions.

'partitionBy' approach would prove helpful when you read back the written data by applying a filter on the basis of 'partitionBy' expression. Because, Spark can then only read the desired sub-directories according to filtering expression leaving the others. However, you should not use 'partitionBy' on data fields having very high cardinality because then it would be result in equally large number of sub-directories.

bucketBy Approach

In this approach, which is also applicable to only Datasets, an additional 'bucketBy' expression along with the number of buckets is also specified in the writer API. Usually, the expression consists of one or more data fields of the Dataset schema. Here , while writing the data records in a partition, for each record, a bucket is calculated first, based on which, the data record is written in a partition and bucket specific file.

Therefore, if a partition can map all its data records to all the available buckets, then the number of files in the primary directory for that partition would be equal to the number of buckets.

In the 'bucketBy' approach, if one also wants to store the bucketing specs then a table name is also additionally specified in the writer APIs. This table would then store the bucketing specs in the table meta space, which can be retrieved during the read operation .

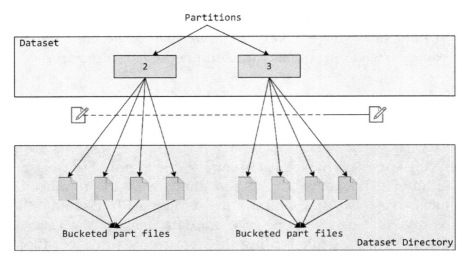

Fig. 5.3: Illustration of using bucketBy approach to write a Dataset on a storage medium

Example 5.3

Dataset 'A' is repartitioned into 2 partitions with schema similar to Example 5.3. 'A's is then written to a snappy compressed parquet format at a specified path using the 5 buckets and 'bucketBy' clause on 'empId' in the writer API. Also, a table is specified in the writer API to store the bucket specification.

```
A = A.repartition(2)
A.write().mode(SaveMode.Overwrite).option("path",
"/usr/poc/example5dot3").bucketBy(5,"dept").saveasTable
("example5dot3");
```

Executing example 5.3 would create a directory example5dot3 at the specified path. Listing the files in the directory would list 10 part files, each of part file corresponds to a single bucket for a single partition. In this example, data records contained in each of partition maps to all the available buckets, therefore, each partition produces 5 partition specific bucket specific files, and hence total 10 part files are created since there are two partitions.

- part-00000-0029823e-1979-483c-8b80-516047109d23_00000.c000.snappy.parquet
- part-00000-0029823e-1979-483c-8b80-516047109d23_00001.c000.snappy.parquet
- part-00000-0029823e-1979-483c-8b80-516047109d23_00002.c000.snappy.parquet
- part-00000-0029823e-1979-483c-8b80-516047109d23_00003.c000.snappy.parquet
- part-00000-0029823e-1979-483c-8b80-516047109d23_00004.c000.snappy.parquet
- part-00001-0029823e-1979-483c-8b80-516047109d23_00000.c000.snappy.parquet
- part-00001-0029823e-1979-483c-8b80-516047109d23_00001.c000.snappy.parquet
- part-00001-0029823e-1979-483c-8b80-516047109d23_00002.c000.snappy.parquet
- part-00001-0029823e-1979-483c-8b80-516047109d23_00003.c000.snappy.parquet
- part-00001-0029823e-1979-483c-8b80-516047109d23_00004.c000.snappy.parquet

In case, some of partitions are not able to map all their data records to all the buckets, then the number of part files would be less than the maximum number of part files i.e., "number of partitions * number of buckets", possible within the writing directory.

Therefore, if your Dataset has a large number of partitions and buckets, the number of files can be drastically large in the writing directory. Hence, it is recommended to repartition the Dataset with the equivalent 'bucketBy' expression into those many number of partitions which is equivalent to the number of buckets. When you apply this recommendation, it would produce in the writing directory the number of files which is equivalent to number of buckets.

'bucketBy' approach gives you a method to preserve your Dataset partitioning on a storage medium such as disk.

Therefore, if you read back your bucketed Dataset from the storage from the corresponding path by specifying the table where the corresponding bucketing specs have been stored, you will end up in having the partitioning semantics which is similar to when you were storing the Dataset earlier. This is of great value, because you can avoid unnecessary re-partitioning of the read Dataset to achieve similar partitioning as was existing before the write.

partitionBy, bucketBy Approach

The 'partitionBy, bucketBy' approach is a combination of individual 'partitionBy' and 'bucketBy' approach. In this approach, both, 'partitionBy' and 'bucketBy' clauses are used in the writer API. However, you have to provide a different expression for 'partitionBy' and 'bucketBy' clauses in the writer API. While writing the data records in a partition, for each of the records, firstly a sub-directory is identified based on the value of 'partitionBy' expression evaluated for the data record. The sub-directory if not present, then the same is created first. After this, the targeted bucket for the data record is calculated, and accordingly the data record is written in the partition and bucket specific file under the identified sub-directory.

Here also, if one also wants to store the bucketing specs then a table name has to be additionally specified in the writer APIs. This table would then store the bucketing specs in the table meta space, which can be retrieved during the read operation

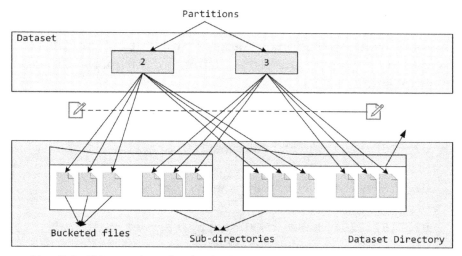

Fig. 5.4: Illustration of using both partitionBy & bucketBy approach to write a Dataset on a storage medium

Example 5.4

Dataset 'A' is repartitioned into 2 partitions with schema similar to Example 5.4. 'A' is then written to a snappy compressed parquet format at a specified path using the partitionBy clause on 'dept', and 'bucketBy' clause on 'empId' with 5 buckets in the writer API. Also, a table is specified in the writer API to store the bucket specification.

```
A = A.repartition(2)
```

```
A.write().mode(SaveMode.Overwrite).option("path",
"/usr/poc/example5dot4").partitionBy('dept').bucketBy(5
,"dept").saveasTable("example5dot4");
```

Executing example 5.4 would create a directory in the targeted filesystem by the name of example5dot4 at the specified path. Listing the files in the directory would list 5 sub-directories as the total number unique 'dept' values across all partitions are 5. In each of the sub directory, there would be 5 bucket specific part files from each of the two partitions.

Therefore, each 'dept' sub directory contains 10 bucketed files in total (from 2 partitions). Therefore, total number of files that would be visible after the listing of primary directory example5dot4 are 50.

- dept=101/part-00000-87c15905-4be4-414a-8656-d7f71671225e_00000.c000.snappy.parquet
- dept=101/part-00001-87c15905-4be4-414a-8656-d7f71671225e_00000.c000.snappy.parquet
- dept=101/part-00000-87c15905-4be4-414a-8656-d7f71671225e_00001.c000.snappy.parquet
- dept=101/part-00001-87c15905-4be4-414a-8656-d7f71671225e_00001.c000.snappy.parquet
- ....
- ....
- dept=105/part-00000-87c15905-4be4-414a-8656-d7f71671225e_00004.c000.snappy.parquet
- dept=105/part-00001-87c15905-4be4-414a-8656-d7f71671225e_00004.c000.snappy.parquet

The combined approach provides benefits of the both the approaches. When you read back a Dataset stored using 'partitionBy bucketBy' approach along with bucketing specs stored in a corresponding table, you could quickly filter the

```
```

data records on the basis of 'partitionBy' expression(s). Further, the filtered records would already be partitioned according to the 'bucketBy' expression therefore avoiding a need of a potential repartition operation.